THE EVOLUTION OF SKATING

WE ROLL WORLDWIDE

VOLUME VII

Amirah Palmer

Printed in the United States of America

Published by
SK8RZ Konnect
5340 Weslayan St., Unit #273323
Houston, Texas 77005
eMail: publisher@sk8rzkonnect.com
Website: www.sk8rzkonnect.com

ISBN: 979-8-9904975-1-1

Library of Congress Control Number: 2022912127

Book Cover and Interior Design:
Jessica Tilles of TWASolutions.com

Special discounts are available on quantity purchases by corporations, associations, educators, and others. For details, contact the publisher.

All SK8RZ Konnect titles are distributed by:
Ingram Content
www.ingramcontent.com

Dedications

After giving honor to Allah (swt) and with heartfelt love and grattitude, I dedicate this book to:

To all those who have believed in, supported, contributed to, and assisted me in creating and sharing this book series, I extend my deepest gratitude. What started as a dream has evolved into a vision, culminating in the manifestation of a book series. Our collective drive has always been to leave a lasting legacy, our legacy, documenting the essence of the skate community and culture in our own words, for the world to see.

I express heartfelt thanks to everyone who has participated in this endeavor, both present contributors and those with future plans to join in shaping this legacy by sharing their journey.

Acknowledgments

"Performance art is about joy, about making something that's so full of kind of a wild joy that you really can't put into words."

–Laurie Anderson

Roller skating transcends being merely a sport; it evolves into an art, a manifestation of personal expression on wheels. Each skater silently communicates the thoughts of their mind, the emotions of their heart, and the unique experiences they wish to share. It's not a skill learned; it's a sensation felt. While there exists a framework of style and rhythm, the individual's expression is distinctly their own.

No two skaters will provide an identical experience. Despite similar moves, the feelings inspiring those actions stem from their unique life journeys. This acknowledgment extends to a remarkable tribe of talented, skilled, educated, and dedicated individuals contributing to this project, both directly and indirectly. In the introspection of 2022, I realized that this book was my dream, and none of you initially signed up for this venture. Yet, collaboratively, we are crafting history, leaving behind a legacy to cherish, all to preserve and safeguard a beloved culture.

Special thanks to those who visually catalog our artistry: Linwood Neverson of Sk8Kingz Media, Doug Mike of Sk8 Vidzz, Terrance Glover of Triple 7 Magazine, Sk8CultureClub, Wes Jiggs, Jayson Vernon, Chad Harrell of SkateLyfe TV, Robert Dea, David Pippen of SkatePhotos.com, Roll Modul, Tyrone Dennis, Malik Thomas of Sk8 Chicago, Scotty Moson, Dr. L. David Stewart of Year60 Photography,

Rogelio Valdez, Kurby Brown, Fabrice Bueno, Chuck Williams of WBSA TV, Debra Chase of Timeless Connections, KappaChris Robinson, Short Shots, Larry Black, Timeless Connections, Glennesha Johnson of DWL Studios, Scott Rinaldi of Scott Rinaldi Photography, Above Ground Photography, Sk8Luv33, Nate Wren, Queen City Skate TV, Ron Fussnecker of Midwest Skaters and the many others who have contributed and are nameless, I thank you and send a wealth of gratitude to you all. Forgive me for those not mentioned. Charge it to my mind and not my heart.

Peace and Blessings to all,

Amirah Palmer

Contents

Preface

"Out of every adversity, comes opportunity."

– Benjamin Franklin

This quote resonates deeply, particularly in the context of the COVID-19 pandemic that forced a significant shift in our daily, work, and social lives. The virus's impact has been profound, rearranging life in unexpected ways. Whether through personal experiences with friends, family, or coworkers, we have all been touched by the pandemic's effects—ranging from early deaths, unemployment, to loneliness and financial instability.

The pandemic prompted a forced stillness, compelling individuals to sit, focus, and recalibrate their lives. It was a moment where the realization of not being in control became apparent. In the silence, people began to grow, reevaluate life from a different perspective, and face the choice of sinking or swimming. Financial struggles were intensified for those already on the brink, and health battles were waged with some facing lingering issues.

The same held true for me. During the pandemic, I hosted a podcast where skaters would visit my studio to share their experiences, history, and passion for roller skating. When quarantined, I had to shift and began conducting interviews via Zoom. As I adapted, a concern crept into my soul—what if this history, our history, is lost? How can I ensure our stories are preserved? Books have always stood the test of time, so I thought of writing a book, a logical choice. But where do I begin? Seeking guidance, I called Ice From Philly, seeking his advice and blessings on this journey. After thorough discussions, he saw the merit in this endeavor and agreed to assist, connecting me with individuals who could contribute to this meaningful project. To him, I am forever grateful.

I aim to take you on a journey into the heart of skate culture, unraveling the passion that fuels our love for the art and sport. This collaborative effort brings together members of the skate community, sharing their stories of introduction, acceptance, growth, and mastery in the artistry and skill of roller skating. I welcome you to immerse yourself in the passion of each contributor, gaining insight into the unique roles we all play in shaping this culture. The evolution of roller skating continues to unfold, offering a versatile experience that can be enjoyed alone or with family and friends. It stands as an inclusive activity, welcoming individuals regardless of race, religion, social, or financial status.

As you delve into each narrative, I encourage you to approach it with an open heart, engage your mind, connect with your soul, and embrace the unfolding journey—the crafty and innovative.

Peace and Blessings

Amirah Palmer

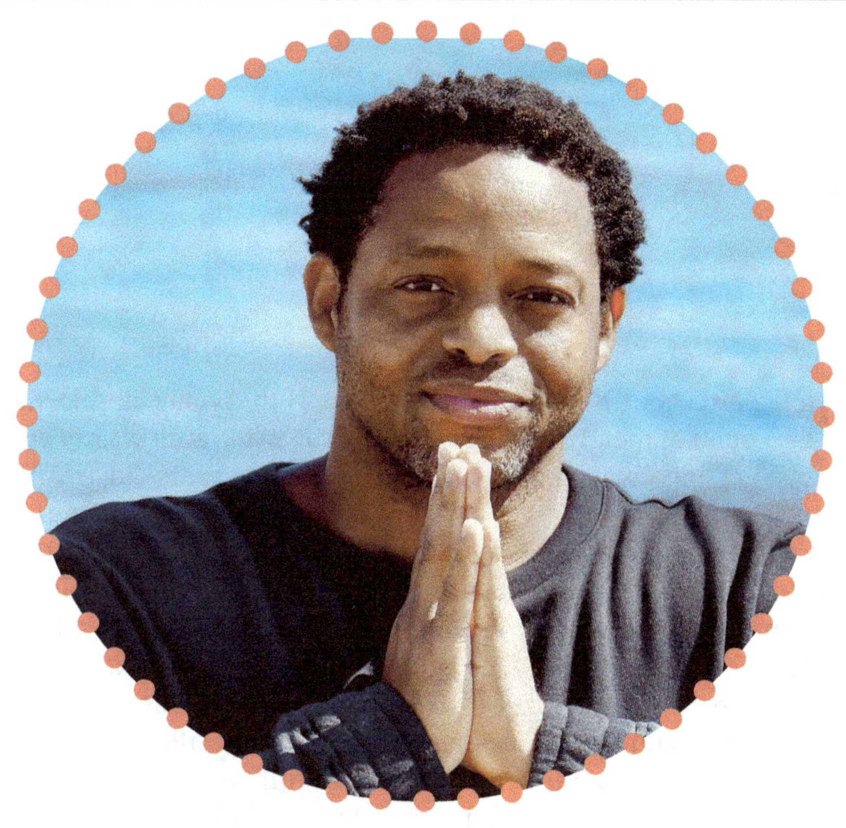

Terrell Ferguson

Facebook: @Terrell Ferguson | Instagram: @TerrellskatesVB

"33 to Venice"

On the streets of South-Central L.A., at 10th Avenue and Denker, the sound of metal scraping concrete was in the air. I wasn't going very fast yet, but I was moving on wheels. At three years old, my mom and dad both worked, so I spent an inordinate amount of time with my grandmother and Paw Paw. They lived in a green apartment with tall stairs. At least, they seemed that way to my three-year-old self. My grandmother didn't work a 9-to-5, but she would take salvaged furniture and clothes, wash and refurbish them, and take it all to the local swap meet to sell. They call that thrifting now. She would pack me up, along with the clothes and small furniture items, in the car (can't remember which brand) and I would roll with her. To keep me from being bored and keep a four-year-old out of mischief, she'd bring my skateboard or roller skates. This was the beginning.

At the swap meets, all the vendors knew my grandmother. Sindy Mae (yes, with an S) was a popular, domineering church figure who demanded respect, and whose presence commanded authority. She had a soft side for me. My dad was the youngest boy, and I was his only son. All of her toughness was melted by my (at that time) innocent face. The community that knew her knew me. They would goad me into skating, biking, or roller skating around the areas, through the customers. It was all entertainment. It must have been pretty good because I could earn a nickel, dime, or quarter if I could roller skate or skateboard under the tables the vendors set up. Your boy was clocking dollars in the entertainment industry at four.

I loved those times at the swap meet and loved my grandmother even more. Anytime someone asks me, "Who taught you how to skate?" I always think back to those times, grandmother on one side,

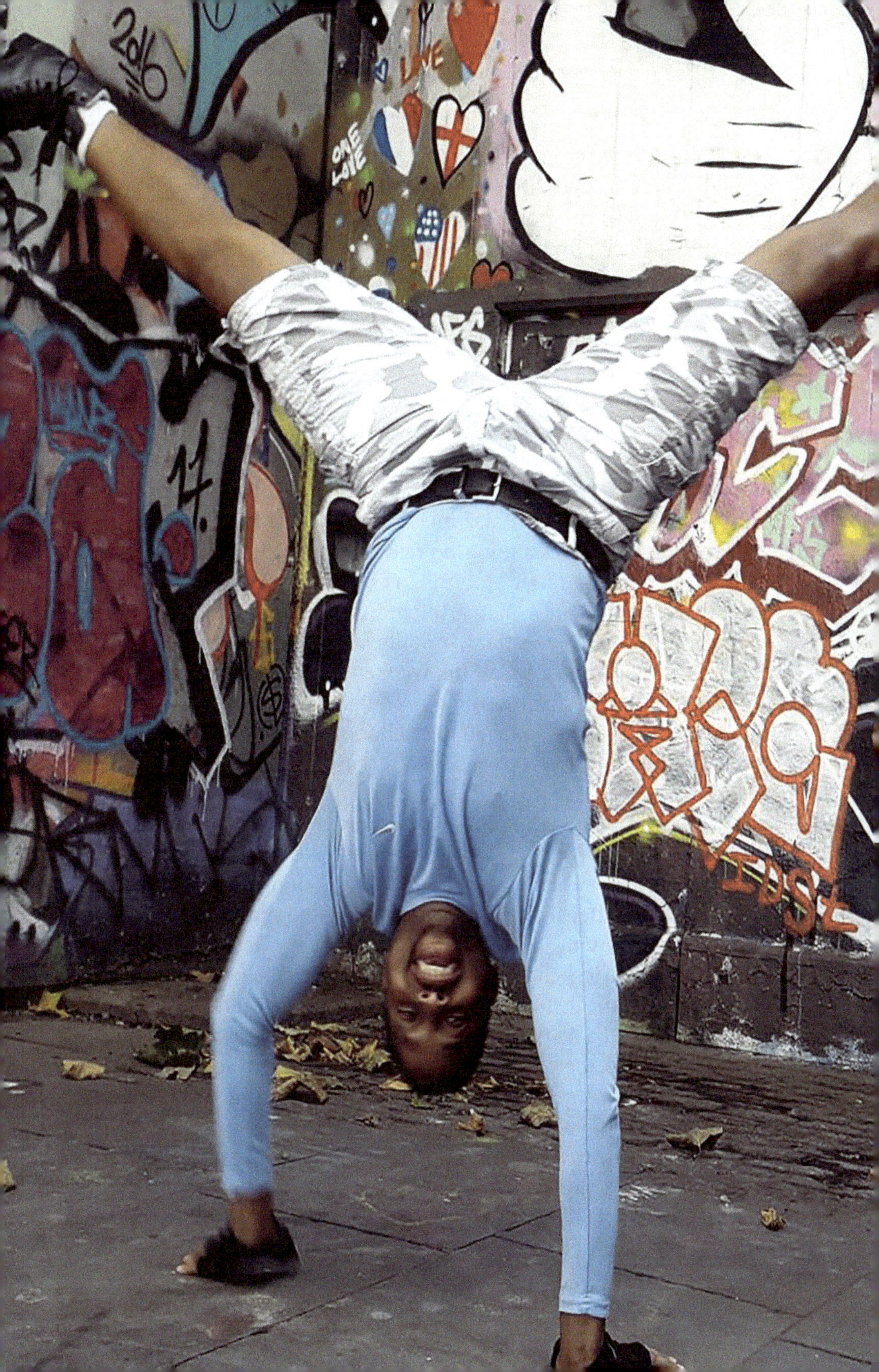
2016
LOVE
ONE LOVE

grandfather on the other, holding my arms as my Bambi-like legs flitted around, trying to keep the wheels under them. Was I good? Nah, not yet, but this was the point where my grandparents were introducing me to the joys of playing outside. We had no video games, Facebook, Instagram, or TikTok. You wanted to communicate with friends, you went outside and played. Being good on a bike, skateboard, or a pair of roller skates (one skate if your friend didn't have a pair) was the way to be popular on the block. I was popular by age nine.

I started school early and later skipped a grade, so I was always smaller than everyone else. At least that's how it felt. My mom and dad divorced when I was three and I didn't handle it well when she remarried when I turned six. It was unofficial, but my dad was an every-other-weekend parent. I missed him…a lot. So, when it was his time to pick me up, assuming he remembered, I was always excited. During my ninth summer on Earth, a couple of months before turning ten, my dad moved into an apartment in Santa Monica. Santa Monica is a five-minute drive, a thirty-minute walk from Venice Beach. My dad was in his prime, so on his weekends, he was still trying to do grown man, in his prime, things. That meant meeting women and shooting hoops. Pops coached me in hoops and I could ball, but when it came to playing with grown men, I was still too small and light in the ass.

Venice Beach was far more well known as a Mecca for Muscle Beach bodybuilding and street basketball during this era, but there was an emerging subculture: roller skating. Young Terrell, at age nine, and already smaller than the other kids, was no match for grown men pushing and shoving on a hoops court, but my dad was not willing to ruin his fun. He heard music playing one weekend at the old skate circle and got an idea that changed my life. The old skate circle was adjacent to the basketball courts. He would allow the skate circle to babysit me while he played basketball. We both got to play. He could hoop and meet women and I would tell my mom I had fun at the beach when he dropped me off at home. Win-Win.

The first time my father dropped me off in the skate circle, he gave me explicit directions, "not to leave." It was the easiest direction he ever gave me to follow. I was inundated with music, people, style, and culture. I couldn't believe my eyes or ears. This has to be what love is.

Nine-year-old me was in heaven. They couldn't have been the first, but Lipps, Inc., "*Funkytown*" and The Gap Band, "*Oops Upside Your Head*" were the first songs I really remember hearing repeatedly. Venice Beach skaters loved The Gap Band. I loved the area and never wanted to leave. The music was funky and nonstop. The people ranged from cool to strange to eclectic to outright weird, and I was there for all of it. Hippies to Hare Krishnas. Every time it was time to go, I sulked. Couldn't wait to go on my own. Skating was the best babysitter ever.

My skates were too big. They had metal wheels and were white, which in non-PC times got me teased by my big OG, *Mad*. Big T, my dad, got the wrong skates rushing out because he was every other weekend, and was as ready as I was to get to the beach. I met Mad in the skate circle when another kid, using the skate circle as a babysitter, got upset with me. She said she was "Gonna get Mad on me." I had no clue who Mad was until I saw him hovering over me at six-foot-three and two hundred thirty-five pounds of pure muscle and scowl. But when I watched him skate, I knew he was going to be the one to teach me how to do what he did. Spins. Flips. Splits. And, oh yeah, meeting women.

My teen years were marked by being shy, awkward, and still short. There was one thing that made them dope. Roller skating. I was still hooping, but basketball at Santa Monica High School was competitive. Not much room for the five-foot-three sophomore. Sitting on the bench, if I was playing at all, was how I spent high school basketball, but there was a place where I wasn't king but I was now the skating prince, under Mad. Venice Beach was now my sanctuary. I was there every weekend. I took the number 33 bus from my moms, straight down Venice Boulevard through four different Crip neighborhoods to get to my spot. I had to be at Venice.

Venice brought out the performer in me. Girls brought out the player. It was a super weird time. In the first part of my teen years, I was shy and didn't even know when girls were flirting, but in my fifteenth summer, I met a nurse named Kim. She and her friend beckoned me over after I did a particularly sexual move, skating. They both laughed when I told them, "I'm almost sixteen." I was insulted by their laughter. Kim was intrigued. Kim returned to Venice solo. This time, she didn't laugh after she beckoned me over. She asked if

I would like to have dinner with her. I told her my best friend, Dan, was coming to pick me up. (Dan and I liked to hang out in Westwood near UCLA, after skating to meet girls.) Plans changed that night. So did my status.

After eating subpar Mexican food, we all went back to Dan's house. I was going anyway because Dan's mom was out of town and that meant me and Dan hanging and trying to find some trouble (lightweight) to get into. But this night, Kim was here. I still didn't realize I was being seduced, but Dan, who was two years older, did. He excused himself upstairs and Kim took my virginity and made me a man. It was FAST. Venice did it again. The woman, six years older than my freshly sixteen-year-old self, had sex with me. Did I mention it was fast?

Now a senior at Santa Monica High School, I had lost my virginity and discovered swagger. (Yes, I was only sixteen as a senior.) Venice had made me a monster. I couldn't hang out with high school girls anymore because Venice Beach was feeding me women. Kim had passed. Technically, she passed herself on to Mad, but that was okay because if it wasn't for him, none of this would have been possible. I love skating. I love what it was doing for me. I love what it was making me. The spins. The flips. The splits. Our crowds were HUGE every weekend and every weekend I took advantage of it by meeting women in the crowd. All of us did. I was a product of watching my dad and Mad. I was learning moves for the love of skating, for the love of women, and for the love of Venice Beach.

I ended my teen years addicted to skating at Venice Beach. There was World on Wheels, Sherman Square Roller Rink, Skate Depot, Skate Land, and others, but I was a Venice skater. I was still not the king, a title which will always be held by Mad, but I was most definitely the man. I couldn't hold down any job or relationship, which required me to miss skating on the weekends. I was attending Cal. State Long Beach and meeting new people and my friends who didn't skate convinced me to start dancing, too. So, I skated by day, ate, showered, and danced by night. Every weekend. All through college. College was difficult because I was extremely busy partying on the weekends and Mad convinced me (didn't take much) to skate Thursday nights at Sherman Square. This whole college thing was getting in the way of my skate/party life. Then Venice struck again. One quiet Saturday rolling, a woman approached me. I thought she wanted to… But she didn't. This woman asked me if I could act. And after careful consideration and deliberation, I said, "Yeah." This was the beginning of my new future.

Now six feet tall and in my twenties, my body had developed. I had friends tell me they'd seen my commercials on TV, which at the time was almost as addicting as skating on Venice. Almost. I was dancing on *Soul Train.* I had friends telling me they loved watching me dance on the train. This, too, was almost as addicting as skating on Venice. Almost. I have a daughter. She's the only thing as important as skating on Venice. She's the only reason I don't freak out if I have to miss a day of skating on Saturday or Sunday. Odd thing though, my daughter does not like skating or Venice. (Am I sure she's mine?) And yeah, even with her, I freaked out sometimes if something she did made me miss a day. I hit twenty-seven and now I have a son, too. He doesn't skate either. Where am I finding these kids? But in reality, they both got my basketball side. But I rarely hoop anymore on weekends at this point because it could interfere with skating at Venice.

Soul Train tapings also drove me nuts. Of course, I wanted to dance on an iconic show that I grew up watching every Saturday morning before going to skate, but why couldn't they shoot on weekdays? I didn't drink. I didn't smoke. My only addiction was skating at Venice Beach. But one of the positive things that *Soul Train* brought on was my skating got better. Moves that I could do dancing I learned to do on wheels, and it added to my range and performance levels.

My twenties were the peak of my powers. I was dancing on tour. I was skating on tour. My style was a combination of ice skating, watching the Olympics because there was no YouTube or TikTok to copy from, and breakdance. After all, *Breakin'* and *Breakin' 2* were filmed on or near Venice and I knew the dancers from the shoot. The only other things that mattered were raising my kids and hooping. This was, by far, the best time of my life.

Venice Beach made me who I am. I'm a prime-time performer because of rolling on that beach. I've been around the world as a dancer and skater. I danced on *Soul Train.* Danced for Michael Jackson. Skated for Madonna. Nothing in my career would be possible without those spins, flips, splits, and tricks. Nothing can replace that feeling. My twenties and thirties were filled with raising kids (now two boys and one girl), shooting commercials, TV or film, and skating at Venice. I had a few jobs here and there, but outside of working as a talent agent, none of them ever mattered, felt right, or stuck. I was made to skate. Dancing and acting (now writing) are by-products of the eight wheels.

Now that I'm older, past my skating prime, and my body is falling apart, I have a new task. My job is to be an ambassador for the wheels and let the younger, new generations know what is possible to achieve. I help younger skaters find work, point them in the direction of agents, managers, and production jobs, and find a way for them to construct careers. I don't really teach as much as I tutor up-and-coming "rollologists" to define and hone their technique and embrace their individuality. That is the one thing about Venice skating that separates it from the rest of the world, the undefined style of performing. Venice skating is all about putting on a show.

As the curtain lowers on my skating, I'm still active in the community. I have a new show streaming on a brand-new platform. The show is *Roll Call*. The platform is TheBrickTV. The show travels from city to city, studying the distinct styles each city brings and how the personality of the city influences the skating and vice versa. We have completed our first season, which included episodes in Los Angeles, The Bay Area, New York, New Jersey, and Atlanta, and a double-episode season finale in Barcelona. Our goal is to bring together the skate community (like this book) and introduce styles, locations, OGs, and newcomers. It shows what's happening today.

I have also written a pilot and five episodes of a TV show called *Ghost Town*, about the early days that shaped Venice Beach roller skating, and the people who were a major part of that formation. (It's looking for a home, TV execs.) And of course, you can still find me skating on weekends at Venice (even though I have to stretch for hours now) when my body cooperates. Even with the pains I go through, I would never change a thing. I love everything that skating has brought me (even the pain) and I am grateful for the direction my life path took because of the eight wheels. (Including my chapter in this book) I plan on riding until the wheels fall off.

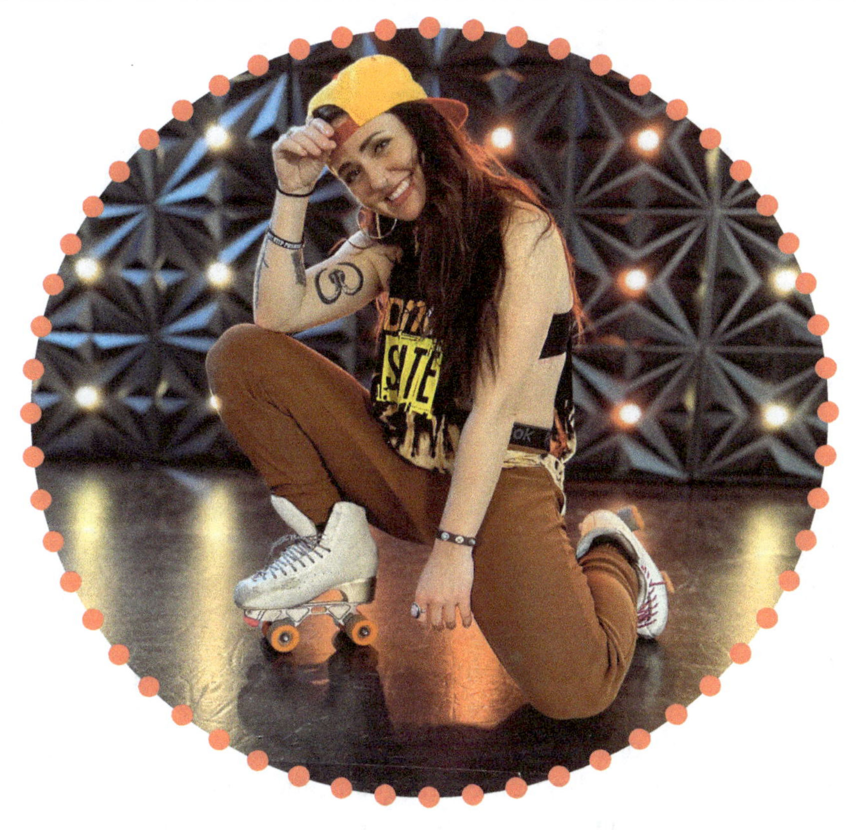

Morgan Weske

Facebook: @Morgan Weske | Instagram: @dance.skate

"Creator of DanceSkate"

Growing up in Tennessee, my love for skating started at the local roller rink, skating several days a week on my first pair of Riedell's at Hamilton Skate Place. Fast forward to 2015, I moved to Los Angeles, where I rediscovered my love for skating!

Growing up as a dancer in Chattanooga, Tennessee, I began choreographing routines at an early age. Immediately after graduating high school, I was offered a position to be a dance instructor, teaching several days a week. I also trained in Atlanta and danced professionally in Nashville. All while dancing, I was serving tables at restaurants and working an office job to support myself financially. During this time, I was also living with a health scare: myelofibrosis. I was diagnosed with an over-productive bone marrow right after high school. I was told from the first two hospitals, "You will only live for five years and never dance again if you didn't go through with the chemo, radiation, and transplant." With an unshakable gift of faith, I knew that wasn't my path and pushed forward with conviction. Fifteen years later, I have lived past my life expectancy. While I am still living with the condition, it lies dormant as I take careful measures to ensure my best quality of life and health. Because of this situation and many more, I started meditating every day. I realized that dance has always been an open door in my life, a door I never had to push open. It just came naturally. I knew that was God's purpose for me. I then moved to Los Angeles to pursue dance on a larger scale in 2015.

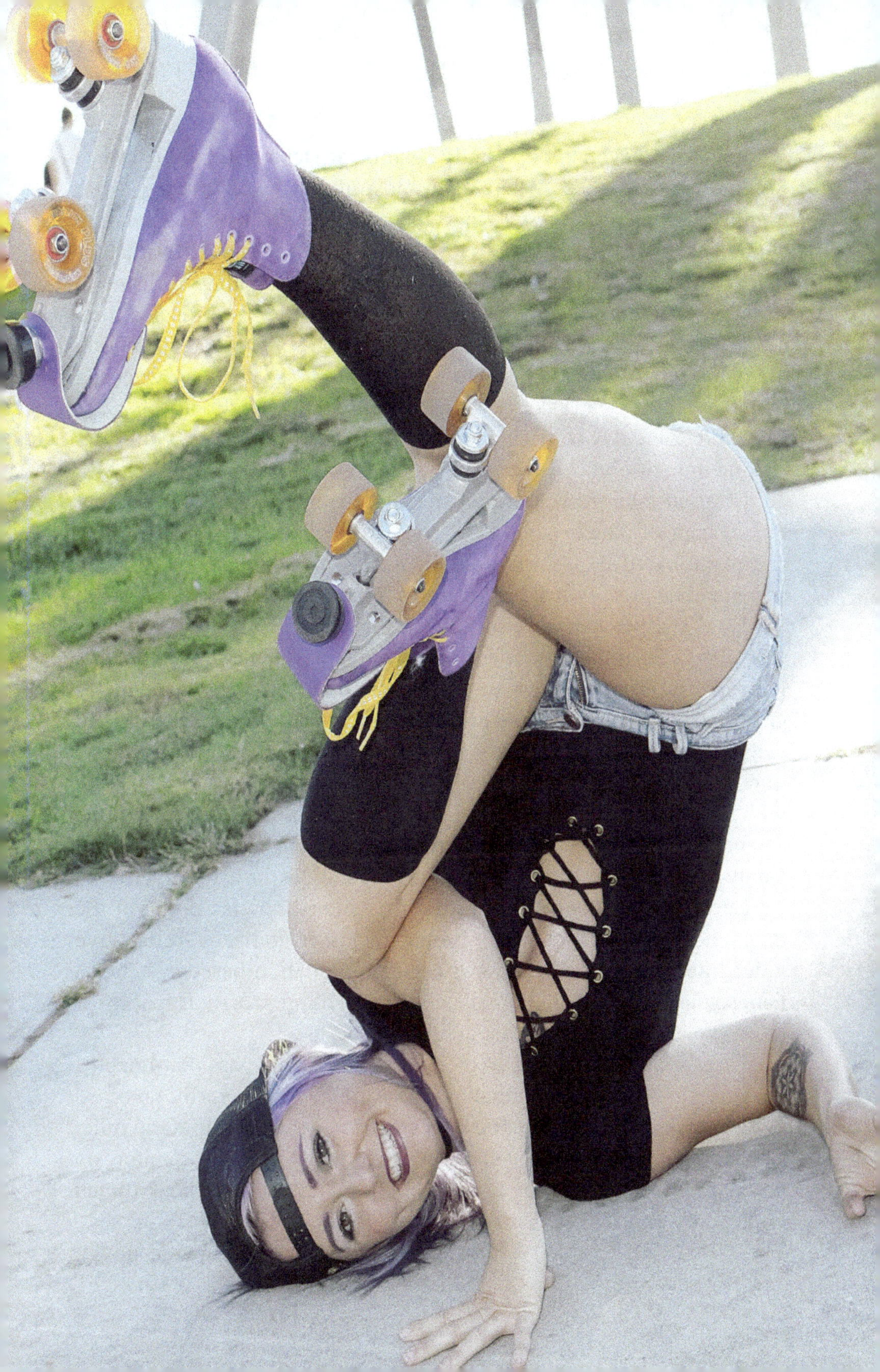

In 2015, I began a work-study position at Debbie Reynolds Dance Studio in Los Angeles, where I did most of my dance training. After training and hustling my way into the dance world, I started going to auditions and doing many live shows and music videos. I performed for the Brian Drake Dance Company, DanceHall Funk, and much more. Within two months, I was choreographing for Warner Records, Inc., and more! While I was having a great time dancing, something kept calling me to the beach. I would drive to the beach to go skate every weekend with the Venice Beach skaters. I discovered them on February 1, 2015. I remember the day so perfectly because I fell back in love with roller skating immensely!

I started taking my roller skates to dance auditions and pitching the concept of dancing on skates to casting directors! Some loved it and some hated it! I started booking more jobs, music videos, and commercials now as a skater, not just a dancer. I fell so in love with Venice that I moved there in 2017 from North Hollywood, where I started my full-time skate lifestyle, teaching private lessons in Venice. I even offered free choreography workshops at the plaza to my girlfriends. Other girls would ask me to teach, but I didn't feel qualified yet. As a trained dancer, I knew I had to put in an ample amount of time to respect the craft and teachers that came before me. After working with Warner Records, Sony, InRage Entertainment, Chosen People, Miguel, DJ Premier, and many more, I taught choreography workshops. I only saw a few teachers teaching skate classes in Los Angeles, so I created a very specific style I didn't see anyone else doing at the time: choreography. Initially, I provided classes gratis, as well as free videography services, until I switched to a donation-based system, as I am so passionate about both dancing and skating. Creating spaces for me to create and give to others fuels my soul!

Fast forward to 2019. I created DanceSkate, my passion project! I am very passionate about dancing and skating, which is why I merged my two loves together. After being recognized online by SureGrip roller skates and skating a lot in Venice, I wanted to put my skate mentors on the map. Using my videography schooling and background, I filmed tutorials by Jimmy Rich and interviews with Dee Upshaw and others. Then, in 2020, Covid-19 hit and turned everything upside down.

Inspired to find creative outlets for people stuck at home, I started making skate challenges with skaters from all over the world! One of my viral videos was The Toilet Paper video, which included over fifty skaters passing around toilet paper on skates. During quarantine, I honored and amplified skaters from the US and beyond by sharing their stories on social media. DanceSkate quickly blew up. Now, I travel a lot and film for my Instagram page.

In 2021, I took my choreography classes to the studio where I have taught dance classes since 2018. I merged the classes into my brand and called them DanceSkate Classes/Workshops. Skaters from other parts of the world inquired about my classes, so I produced Dance Skate Workshops in other cities. Creating my own flyers, website, and ticket links, I did it all. I modeled my classes exactly from the dance industry, from where I am credited. Inspired to expand DanceSkate and travel, I lived nomadically for two-and-a-half years out of a suitcase and edited for freelance jobs remotely. I taught DanceSkate Workshops throughout Central America, Europe, and all over the United States. I have now taught in over eight countries and fifty cities!

I traveled throughout 2020-2022, but in January 2023, I moved back to Venice Beach and back into a new apartment. I'm not slowing down my travels, but my nomadic two-and-a-half years of traveling out of a suitcase ended. I plan to get back into the entertainment industry, even more, this time, where I once was before Covid-19 happened. However, this time, working on more sets as a creative director and choreographer than I did before. I love skating and dancing with a passion. Skating since 1998, a lifestyle since 2015, and living out of a suitcase to afford to travel to skate parties all over the globe, I will never stop dancing and skating. I will find a means to afford it and make it my lifestyle one way or the other. When life gives you five years to live, that makes you reevaluate your life. I was told I might not live long, so I quickly realized life isn't about money, but about doing something every day that makes you happy, because tomorrow isn't promised. So... go skate today!

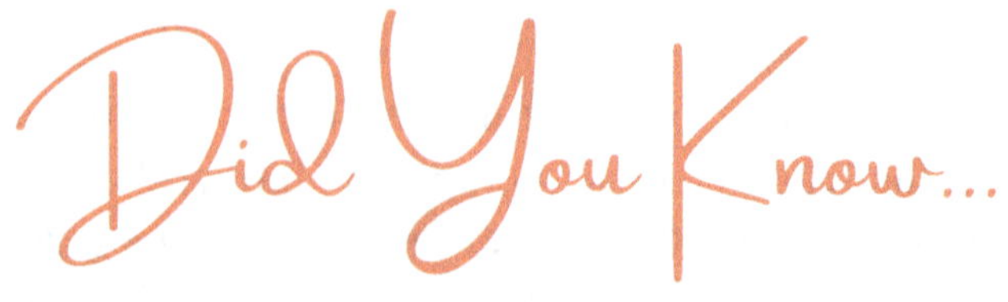

Drive-ins and Roller Skates

The experience of going to a drive-in for a meal of burgers and fries held a special charm for Boomer kids in numerous ways. Firstly, the simple pleasure of biting into a juicy hamburger, crispy fries, and sipping on a creamy milkshake was akin to tasting a slice of heaven. The combination of flavors and textures created a memorable culinary experience that lingered on the taste buds long after the meal was finished.

Secondly, the novelty of eating in the comfort of one's own car added an element of excitement and fun to the dining experience. Sitting behind the wheel or reclining in the passenger seat, families could enjoy their meal while basking in the privacy and coziness of their vehicle. It was a departure from traditional dining settings and offered a sense of freedom and informality that appealed to both children and adults alike.

However, what truly elevated the drive-in experience to a whole new level of enjoyment was the sight of cute teenage girls gliding effortlessly on roller skates, delivering trays of delicious food right to the car window. This charming touch added an element of nostalgia and whimsy to the dining experience, transforming a simple meal into a memorable event. For Boomer kids, the sight of these roller-skating carhops was synonymous with good times and carefree moments spent with family and friends.

The drive-in concept itself traces its origins back to 1921, when two enterprising individuals, J.G. Kirby and R.W. Jackson, recognized the burgeoning popularity of automobiles in Dallas, Texas. Sensing an opportunity to cater to the needs of car owners who preferred the convenience of dining without leaving their vehicles, they opened the first-ever drive-in restaurant called the Pig Stand. This pioneering establishment laid the foundation for a culinary phenomenon that would captivate generations of Americans and become an iconic symbol of American dining culture.

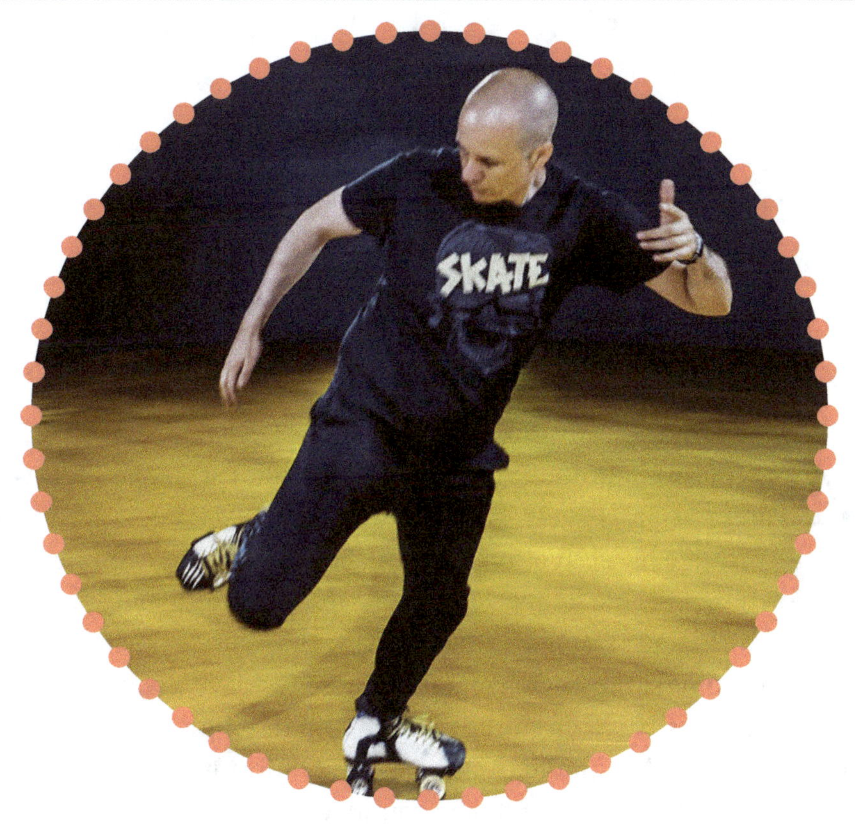

Chad Lankford

FaceBook: @Chad Lankford | Instagram: @chad_lankford

"Truth About Me—Explanations"

My name is Chad Lankford, and I am addicted to skating. My skating style is well… let's say unique. My hips' ability to externally rotate is above average. Although with that comes the limitation of being able to internally rotate less than the average person. When I am skating, I prefer to be either in side stance position or on one foot at a time. I travel on average two to three days a week to skate. My drive time is between thirty minutes and three-plus hours. Why? Because I live in the middle of nowhere and unfortunately, rinks have always been sparse by me and they continue to dwindle. More on that later on. The closest rink to me and the rink I grew up skating at is Skateland Canton in Canton, Illinois. I skate with my entire family at least once a week. My wife and two daughters also enjoy skating… perhaps not as much as I do…but that's understandable. The rest of the time I either travel alone to go skate or meet up with many friends who I have met through this lifestyle.

I believe my inherent side stance comes from my grandfather. I used to visit my grandparents most weekends. As I was growing up, I would follow my grandfather around and, as children do, I would imitate everything subconsciously. My grandfather was Military Police in World War II. As such one of his jobs was to go after people running from the fighting or going AWOL. During one of these events, he chased one of the soldiers under barbed wire and into an apparent minefield. A mine went off, shattering my grandfather's leg. The

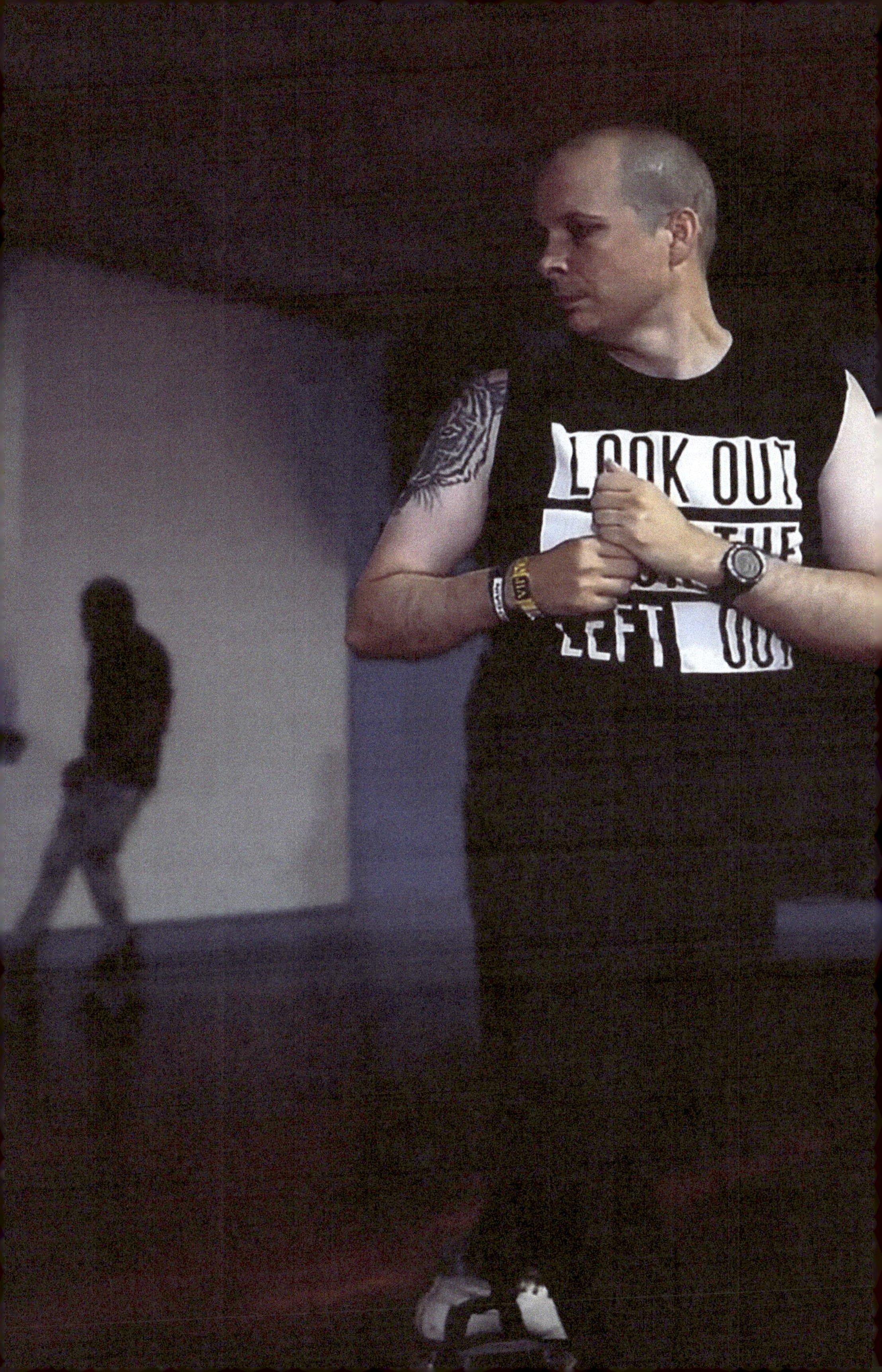
LOOK OUT

nurses put his leg back together the best they could. However, a lasting effect of this was the fact that his gait was affected. He would, for the rest of his life, walk with an outward gait. As such I imitated what I saw, which meant as my muscles were developing, I was also walking with an outward gait. I am sure I looked like a little penguin following this man around his yard all day. While I have no medical evidence, I truly believe this affected my hips and allows for such external rotation. I love this man very much; he has long since passed, but he has had and will continue to have a lasting effect on my life in so many ways.

Growing up in the middle of nowhere and in the country led to many days of boredom. There was never much to do and going to see my friends meant walking five miles along the no-longer-in-use railroad track or riding my bike along the edge of the “busy” highway into town. Luckily, as a teenager, I discovered my love of skating. It started out in the normal way…it was the weekend we were bored and we needed something to do. Growing up in the country meant you had to travel to do anything. Call up your friends, make plans, and see whose parent wanted to drive us somewhere. For me, most of the time was spent with my best friend Shaun, and his mother did most of the driving. We started hitting the local rink around the age of thirteen or fourteen. Generally on a Friday or Saturday night. Doing the normal teenager things, chasing each other on the floor, trying to show off for any girls who might be there that night and, of course, not listening to the rules. This went on well into high school and into my late teens. Although the ability to listen to the rules came as it usually does with maturity. Back then it was a time killer, something to do, but it always felt different to me. Everyone seemed to enjoy skating; but myself, I craved it. Something about the freedom of the skate floor, the lights, the sounds, it all just made the rest of the world disappear.

We had a few decent skaters back then that would go out to the center and do tricks…it was like watching another world. I would get lost in it and watch when the rest of my friends would be off messing around. I don’t think I ever knew just what was going on back then, but I think my future was before me, even if I did not know it. The rewiring of my brain was occurring, although I would not realize this until many years later. During this time, I also met the love of my life and my future wife. We knew each other for a while before dating, and wouldn't you know it, our first date was at the local skating rink. She completes me and for a while, life happened. We both got jobs and went to college. As time went by, the skating rink faded into a wonderful memory. Somewhere along the way, we moved in together, got married, and had two wonderful daughters. My life felt complete… but little did I know one thing was missing and would soon come front and center once again.

Fast forward to April 2, 2016. Little did I know my life was about to change and would never be the same. I had started a weight loss routine several months earlier and decided my kids were old enough, nine and seven, to take them out roller skating. It's great exercise, and I enjoyed it so much in my teenage years. It was time to try it as a family. The first night I was rusty as I expected, but the entire family enjoyed it. We did not have Skate Mates so I was literally holding the kids up by their arms as they learned and got their footing. From then on, we began going weekly. Before I knew it, the kids were skating on their own. Soon enough, I had bought my own skates; then skates for the kids and wife. Before you knew it, a year or so had gone by and I was down from two hundred eight-five pounds at my peak weight to my lowest point of one hundred seventy-seven pounds. I felt amazing both physically and mentally. Skating may not have been the only reason for the weight loss, but it definitely helped. Diet and good exercise are key and, of course, caloric deficit. I had found my place, my peace, my rejuvenation.

In April 2017, the decision was made. I had been doing this for a year and I planned to keep doing this until my death. It was time for an upgrade. I ditched the cheap beginner skates I had bought and started working on a new plan. After much research, I settled on my new setup. With the help of many friends in the community, I saw my skate dream build come to life. To this day, these are my go-to skates—to the point of later having them tattooed onto my arm: Antik

AR1 (Black and White and Gold Foil Color Lab), Snyder Advantage Plate, Custom Black and White Wicked Scott (Scott Corey) Wheels, Ceramic Bearings, and Plugs. Along with the new skates, I also ordered a ZUCA tiger print bag with my name on the front and created a toolkit to house all the extras with my skates in the new bag. Within thirty minutes of being on the floor with my new boots, I knew I would not be going back to a heeled design. It was like this boot was made for my foot and this setup only helped to accentuate my sideways style of skating—I was doing things I did not know I could do and pushing new boundaries. While other skate setups have come into my life and still reside on my wall, nothing compares to my Antik. At the time of writing this, I believe I own sixteen unique sets of skates in my size.

My affinity toward skating sideways began as a teenager and is still there and very apparent. I have always been told to "Take what you're good at and go for it." I sought ways to improve myself and looked for others doing the same in the skating world. I found a group called the Quad City Cuttaz in East Moline, Illinois. It was a one-and-a-half-hour drive for me, but I decided I would go every Wednesday. I have some social anxiety, so for the first few sessions, I did my thing, kept my distance, and watched. Their style of skating was not something I was used to. It was my first introduction to JB skating. After a few weeks, I introduced myself, or should I say they introduced themselves, as I was afraid to approach them. The group provided both the motivation and the training I was looking for. It was apparent my skating style did not match theirs, but it did not matter. We skated together. I became a member of their group and we were family.

In June 2019, I visited someone I had met online. Doc SK8, as he was known in the SkateLogForum, was very influential in everything I had learned over the years. His articles would lead to my desire for more and more skating knowledge. I boarded a plane with my oldest daughter and we flew to meet the man himself, Fred Benjamin (aka Doc SK8). Fred was even more amazing in person. To this day, I have found no one with his level of knowledge when it comes to skating. He blew my mind the couple of days we spent in his shop. I was a sponge, soaking up every bit of knowledge I could understand and even some I would have to look into, as this man is brilliant. When all was said and done, I had made a friend and someone I still look up to and admire. This man has always shot straight with me over the years, and I hope he knows how much his time and friendship mean to me. During that trip, something else substantial also happened. My oldest daughter, who I would say most resembles me in behavior and mannerism, got herself a new set of skates. I paid for half and she paid the other half. A custom set of skates built by the man himself. A NOS Riedell 395 with a customized PowerTrac plate and cannibal wheels. To this day, I think she made her feet stop growing. As she continued to get taller, her feet never grew, and she still skates this setup and I think she will for the rest of her life. That trip will be talked about long after I have left this world—of that, I am sure.

Over the next few years, I would continue to improve and hone my skills. We would travel farther and farther to find rinks we had yet to visit. Every year when we went on vacation, the first thing added to the packing list was our skates. It did not matter if we were driving or flying, those skates were coming. It's amazing to roll into any new rink and see the people and the love and joy in that place. To get onto that new floor, do a few laps and dial in—feel the floor: is it grippy, loose, or somewhere in between? You have to find that breakpoint—how fast can I take a corner sideways before it feels like my wheels are breaking loose or the slide is starting to happen? Those first few laps will dictate how I skate for the night or what adjustments I should make. Tighten trucks, loosen trucks, different wheels, etc. It's always fun skating in a new rink, especially in smaller towns.

There are some nice rinks out there in the middle of nowhere small-town America. It always feels good to get asked questions or receive compliments from both kids and adults alike. It makes me feel like I am doing something right. Like I am influencing people at that rink. I always try to encourage any adults that see me or ask about skating. You are never too old to get back out there. If you want to wear safety equipment, that's fine. Do you. If it's a love or a passion, you will know it. I enjoy skating public sessions as much as adult nights. The children are the future. We need to pass on this love, this passion, and this knowledge onto them. Without the next generation, we will have nothing left. Anytime I can be on the skate floor, I am at my best.

Over the years, I have also skated in many big towns: Chicago, Illinois; St Louis, Missouri; Orlando, Florida; Cleveland, Ohio; San Antonio, Texas and likely more I am forgetting. However, Chicago has always felt like a second home. My first experience in Chicago was when my wife and I, along with some friends, took a class with none other than the Smooth Goddess herself, Myesha McCaskill (https://www.inspiredbyfavor.org). Her class and her team were nothing short of amazing. She welcomed us with open arms and continues to greet me by name anytime we run into one another.

Later that same year, I decided I would try my first national event. Independence Roll X in Chicago. I knew it was going to be amazing the minute I stepped into the building. I had occasionally spoken to Josh Smith, aka Batsmoke, online and when we met in person, he hugged me and told me, "Welcome home." Nothing could have meant more. We later talked while he was lacing up one night and instilled some of his wisdom in me (https://www.batsmokeent.com). I also met Malik Thomas at that event and many other well-known skaters I had only seen online. Everyone was so welcoming and nice. People who skate are like family and they have always welcomed me wherever I go and it has meant a lot to me through the years.

The next year at Independence Roll XI was just as amazing. Malik is an amazing videographer and always captures the event with a skill I cannot believe. I was even lucky enough to be featured on his JBSkateChicago Instagram page (https://jbskatechicago.com). The comments from the over sixty-five thousand views on my reel were amazing and truly have helped me to be less socially awkward and willing to be more open and talk to more people. Much more than I have ever been in the past. Chicago is and will always be a second home to me thanks to all the people I have met and the amazing amount of love felt during each visit. A special shout out and thank you to Jessica

Stroud and D-Breez Darius for always having an amazing gathering at Independence Roll in Chicago each year. I am sure without both of you and many others, this event would not happen.

Cut to the present day. Where am I in my life? I continue to skate two to three days a week. I took my style and my skill and I refined it into what you see today—something unique. I continue to push my boundaries and expand my skill set. I am affiliated with two different local skate groups: Old Fools Sk8 Crew based out of the Quad Cities (Rock Island, Illinois;Moline, Illinois; Davenport, Iowa; Bettendorf, Iowa) and P-Town Rollerz based out of Peoria, Illinois. If you are ever near either location or just anywhere nearby, come check us out. We are always looking for new people to roll with us. I am full bore and have my skates tattooed on my upper left arm hoping to do a full skate-related sleeve. The right arm has a white tiger which represents me and the rest of the soon-to-be sleeve on that arm will have an animal, each chosen by and used to represent my wife and two daughters. Both sleeves are and will be UV tattooed as well. It just felt needed…so many black lights in most skating rinks.

If you have questions about me or skating in general, feel free to reach out on Facebook. Finally, some words that I hope will come across as wisdom: Live each day to the fullest. If you find something you are passionate about, embrace it with everything you have. Support your local skating rinks. Rinks are not an easy business to be in and have many expenses. The best rinks are the rinks run by skaters who have the same passion for the sport. In the seven years since I have returned to skating, more than a dozen rinks within driving distance of me have closed. We have some very large cities left without rinks and there is no good reason for this. Support your local rink. If you blink, it could be gone. If you know of a local rink for sale, reach out and help them find that buyer who will keep it a rink. Spread the word—all it takes is time and you could save not just a rink but a community; a lifestyle. Family is everything, whether it's by blood or by love. Skate family is no exception. Treat others with respect. Enjoy what you do. Skate whenever you can, whether that's a public skate, an adult night, or a national event. Always remember the youth are the future. Reach out to them, teach them, mold them, and embrace them. To everyone who has been by my side during my journey, I appreciate every one of you and to those I have yet to meet or will eventually meet in this passion we call skating, Much Love…

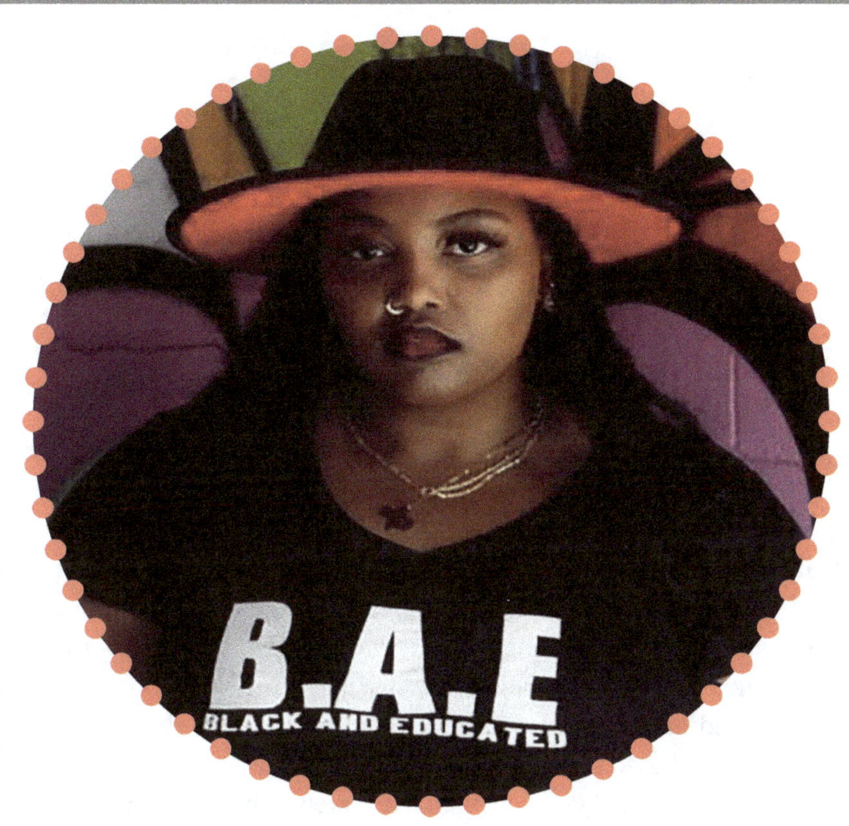

CeCe Altius

aka H-Town Diva

Facebook: @CeCe Altius | Facebook: @getem_cece

"It's Not a Hobby. It's a Lifestyle"

Houston, Texas, is my home. I come from a family of veterans, athletes, and business owners. Having a business owner as a mother granted me an adventurous childhood. My mother was the founder and CEO of an astonishing youth care center in the city of Houston. Field trips were a must for us, from water parks, zoos, museums, and amusement parks to even trips across the U.S.A. But for me, none of those field trips compared to a day at the skating rink. From the smell of old wood mixed with nacho cheese from the snack bar and distressed skates to the neon-painted walls, no-lock restroom stalls, and the showcase where you could rent speed skates, light-up chains, and pacifiers.

I remember seeing photos of me in a bassinet on the side of the rink propped up so I could watch everyone skate. Little did I know, in a few years, that would be me out there on the floor. At the time, I attended Starlight Skating Rink, which later became The Zenith Roller Rink (The Z). That rink really birthed and raised me. I went from the bassinet, walking on the rink floor, wearing the plastic in-shoe Barbie skates to being a brownie, which we true skaters call skate rentals, then to an official owner of my own skates. I'll never forget that one Christmas, my older brother gifted me my first pair of skates. From that point on, I was determined to master what my brother and his friends did on skates and advance to higher levels. It wasn't long before I became a "rink rat."

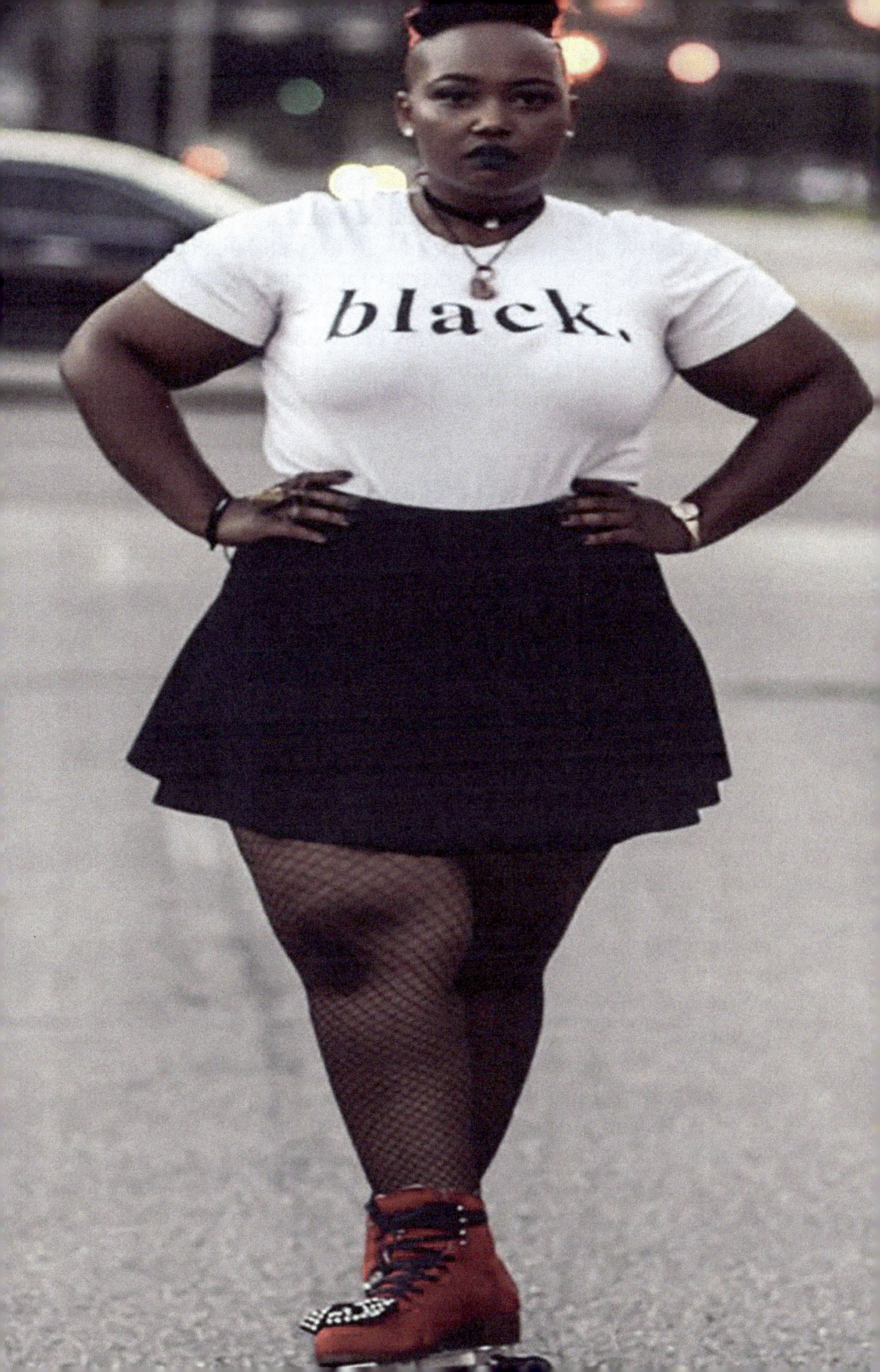
black.

I was at the rink a minimum of four days out of the week. If the rink was open, I would try to be there. I was told if I kept my grades up and stayed out of trouble, I would be able to roll. My mother was very protective and stern but believed in a well-balanced lifestyle. Like any mother, she wanted the best for me and was willing to do whatever to keep me sensible. I made sure to keep that same mindset she programmed over the years of my life; work hard first, play later. It became such a habit I started incorporating it into skating by focusing on the technique itself and then once I got it, I would add my own flavor and play around with it.

Before I knew it, the two were inseparable. Skating had become more than a hobby. It was a priority for me because of the positive influence that came from it. I was bullied as a kid, so in addition to athletics and martial arts, skating gave me confidence, courage, and a voice. I never knew how much I had held in over the years of being attacked about the way I looked, my hair, my size, or just being me until I skated. I would skate so hard and be drenched in sweat like I had just come from swimming. There had been times I would hear a song that I enjoyed, and my mind would go blank where my body would free-flow like a bed of water, and my skates would talk for me. In a sense, it's like being hypnotized and the beat of the music is narrating to you what to do.

I've had some intense skating sessions, but I wouldn't trade them for anything. Some of those fragile moments brought some of the best skate family I needed in my life. Whether when I had broken my leg/ankle, I was in between jobs, didn't know where I would lay my head, or struggling mentally to keep faith in God, my skate family was there, better than some of my blood family. Skate family is true family away from home. I have mother and father figures, aunts and uncles, a lot of brothers and sisters, but most of all, people who really love and care about me. Skating gave me an extended family who I could trust and gain a lot from. I had realized sometimes in life there were going to be obstacles and gaps that needed filling and God knew exactly what (skating) and who (skate family) to put in place of those gaps and adversities. All of my skate family is important to me whether they are indoor or outdoor skaters. They make skating that much more of an enjoyment.

How grand is it to connect with others who share the same love for skating as me? But that's not all we are. We are skaters by skaters night, but by day, we may be photographers, fitness trainers, therapists, tax consultants, barbers, stylists, musicians, graphic designers, real estate agents, ministers, doctors, truck drivers, and the list goes on. We all can instill something in one another no matter the age, gender, profession, or skate style. This explains why I respect the OGs and seasoned skaters who paved the way for me and the next generations to come so much. If it weren't for them, we wouldn't have what we have now as a skate community, let alone the wisdom I've gained from them. But I also acknowledge and credit the new generations for the intense energy they pour out that keeps everyone going. My skate family is the icing on the skate cake. It's important to surround yourself with positive, sincere individuals who educate and support you.

Through maturation, I developed a career in medical and healthcare studies, became a published model and actress, an inspiring recreational sportswoman and skate coach. Each was significant to the skater that I am, but even better than the person I am today. With experience in these fields, I convey patience and aid to new and senior skaters and broadcast healthy self-assurance as we all should have, and support positive rivalry to keep pushing ourselves to the next level of greatness. As in any act, as a skater in the skate community, you create your own reputation. And for some, they couldn't care less about that, but for me, I did and still do because I know how I want to be treated and where I am trying to go with my skates. I've aimed to be my true authentic self, that friendly social butterfly who will hype up anybody I encounter. You never know who's watching or what someone may be going through. Skating has not only changed many people's lives but saved them, including mine. I could have been doing God knows what, but skating gave me a reason to be a better me. You can ask any true skater with a low vibrational background, and I guarantee they'll tell you, "Man, if it wasn't for skating, I don't know where I'd be." Sometimes, skating was all I had, and I was okay with that.

It taught me to be appreciative of what I have. I knew my skates wouldn't lie to me; they would always be there. What I gave to them, they would give back to me and they gave me life. People will say I'm sensitive, and I'll say you're damn right I'm sensitive about skating, and about my skates. You have no idea what I've been through to be standing where I am today because of God and this gift He has blessed me with. I'm so passionate about it. I knew the end of a relationship I was in was coming when my boyfriend at the time said skating was childish. I must have lost my mind that day. But that just helped me understand that skating is not for everybody, and everyone is not going to understand what skating means to me.

While ripening, I was able to deepen the meaning of why I skate. I propelled myself toward skating in parades, skate parks, trails, and other community and social events that welcomed me and my skates. I got to see how skating outside improved my skating skills and even how it was beneficial for my health. I loved the fact that participating in events sparked up so much good energy and stimulating feedback. It's like people had forgotten or thought skating was dead, but when they saw us, it brought them back to the good old days. We'd hear so many stories of how they used to skate or when they had the best birthday party at the skating rink, or they didn't know skating was so modern. Skating has always brought out the good in everything in my eyes, even myself. It helped me smile more, be social, be okay with not being okay, and give a reason for life.

Skating will forever be a part of me and my life. Even if I'm sprouting grays, losing teeth, or walking with a cane, I assure you I'll be skating. I've come a long way. I've conquered a wide genre of skating, skills, and techniques. I have come across so many beautiful people and learned a lot, but I still have more I'd like to accomplish, especially with the youth and neighborhood communities. I encourage others to give skating a shot. Try it out and see what it can do for you. I want people to know that you can learn to skate and acquire healthy life-coping skills through it, whether it's mental or physical. Skating is all about the connection you have with yourself, your skates, and what you can give back to others from it.

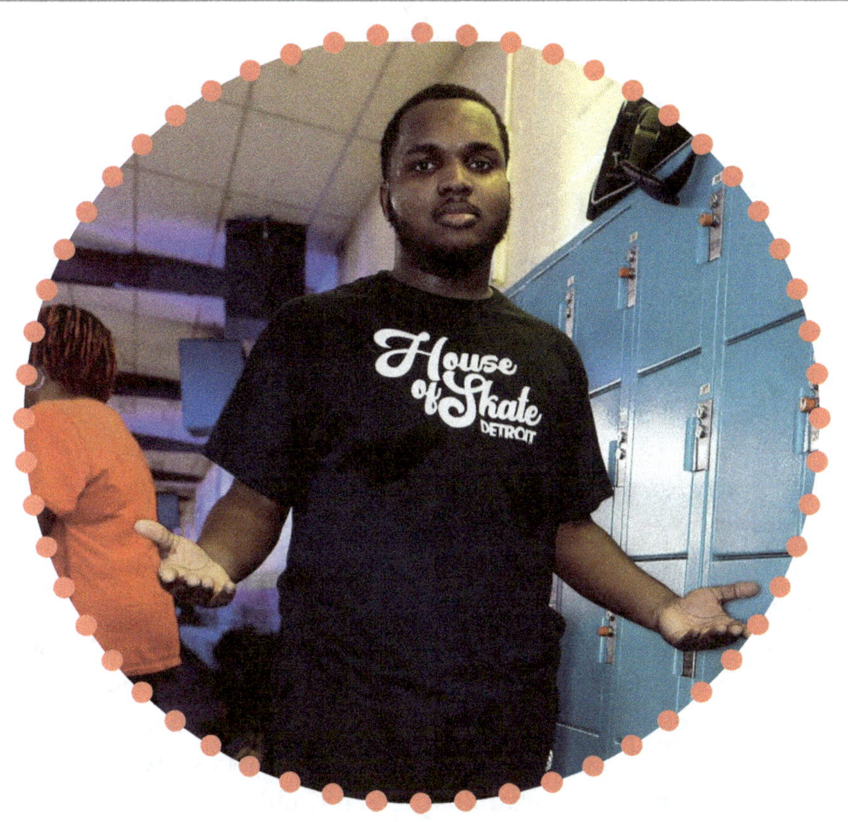

Elijah Smith

Facebook: @Elijah Smith | Facebook: @ hsfskatepage

"Visions Into Reality…A Skate Journey"

Growing up, a lot of things didn't come easy for me. When I say this, I say it not from a point of struggle but more a mental standpoint. I was diagnosed with Attention Deficit/Hyperactivity Disorder (ADHD) Although it doesn't affect many, I caught the worst of it. While I learned to adapt to it in my personal life, once I started skating, it definitely felt like I had to start a whole new chapter in my life! You wouldn't believe how much roller skating has changed my life. Something that started as a hangout with me and my friends has turned into a lifestyle. From building friendships and connections and creating a safe place, even being able to start my own business! I definitely owe it to skating. It has changed my life for the better. Starting with teaching myself moves to the people and connections I have met along the way. Skating has provided a safe place for me to shine with my disability.

It all started back in the summer of 2018, just going into high school. Some friends and I wanted to find something to do. It all started on a Wednesday night. My friend and I were going to a regular family session, but to our surprise, they had the time listed wrong on Google. When we arrived, it was the start of a Detroit Style Skate Class. During the class, I found it was very difficult to learn; it seemed like it was one of the hardest things to learn. Everything was new to me and it was hard to focus on the moves and the beat with my ADHD.

The Detroit Style requires you to catch, ride the beat and stay on count. The instructor kept telling me repeatedly to focus (of course,

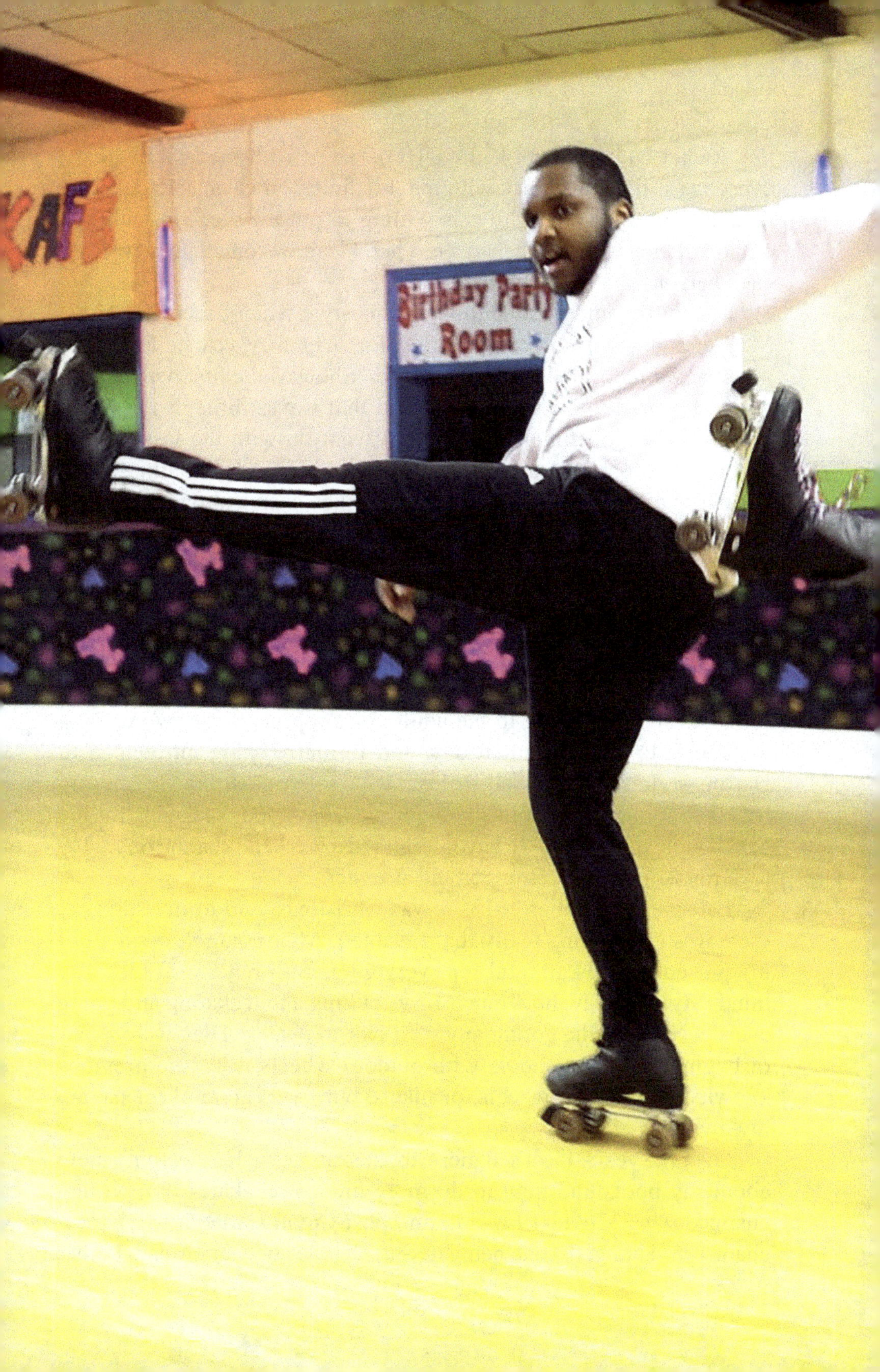
Birthday Party
Room

the teacher had no idea I had ADHD). Even with the lack of focus, everyone still had patience with me. I definitely owe an abundance of thanks to every skater who was willing to put the work in with me. Although I never officially had a teacher, I learned something new from each person who rolled with me.

I knew I would be able to learn this style when I met Ms. Angie McClendon. She has been skating for over fifty years. From the moment we met, she was vested in me. She was the first person with whom I shared that I had ADHD and that it was difficult for me to learn. She didn't flinch. She simply went on with the lessons and told me, "Look forward and listen to the beat. You've got this." She has never treated me differently, and she has been a strong mentor in my learning. I also learned from and want to thank Ms. Cynthia, Ms. Trenaye, Edward, Kenny Nate, Ramone Rob and Darnell for extending the same understanding and grace. I never had a one-on-one teacher, yet I learned something from everyone who took time with me. After participating in the class, there was an adult session afterward, and it was a whole new scene of skating. I was used to attending the kids and teens sessions, so going to the adult session brought a new meaning to skating to me. After that day, and formally being introduced to Detroit-style skating, I fell in love with roller skating. Me and my friend continued to visit this rink for weekdays and weekends for the next couple of months, we haven't missed a weekend skating once. My love for skating grew stronger and stronger.

Later, in December 2018, it was Christmas, and to my surprise, there wasn't anything really that I wanted. After going through all of my presents, I was grateful for everything, but my last gift blew my mind. My mom saw how much I was talking about skating and going every weekend. She got me my own pair of skates! They were a pair of beginner Chicago boots with outdoor wheels. I had no previous knowledge of boots, wheels, or plates, but I was grateful for having my own pair of skates.

Over the years, I learned more about skating, such as learning more about my boots and how to do more moves on skates. Everything changed when Covid-19 had it, and post-Covid started a whole new chapter in skating, despite being new to Detroit-style, my friend, Lamar and I, who would eventually become my business partner, created HSFSkatepage (House of Skate and Friends), a roller skating page on Instagram.

We started the page to showcase a side of skaters that didn't get recognition for their skills or progression. Other skate pages showed popularity over skills, it seemed like, and some posts didn't give skating a good representation. Little did I know, everything that happened in that single month had changed a lot for the year.

Growing my skills as a skater and a videographer, with only two months into learning Detroit-style, there were only a few rinks where I could skate. Then on February 26, 2022, Kyle Black, the owner of Rollercade, reached out to ask me about working together. With my roller skating page being new and still less than five hundred followers, it was a blessing. Experiencing a new skating rink with new skaters showed me more people that had the same love of skating that I had. Even with the few events I had worked on as a videographer, it carried along throughout the year, allowing me to explore new rinks and meet new people. The original two rinks that I would go to at the beginning of the year turned into ten, which I would rotate around through the end of the summer!

While my skating journey is still only officially starting with me being two years in now, I have a lot planned. From meeting new people in and out of town, learning more from skating on and off the rink, and even growing myself as a videographer and watching myself progress there. I plan on doing this for a long time, so I'm going to keep on putting in the work and have the same love I started with and more at that! With time, effort, and practice, I believe everyone who loves this art/sport can put the work into becoming great at it.

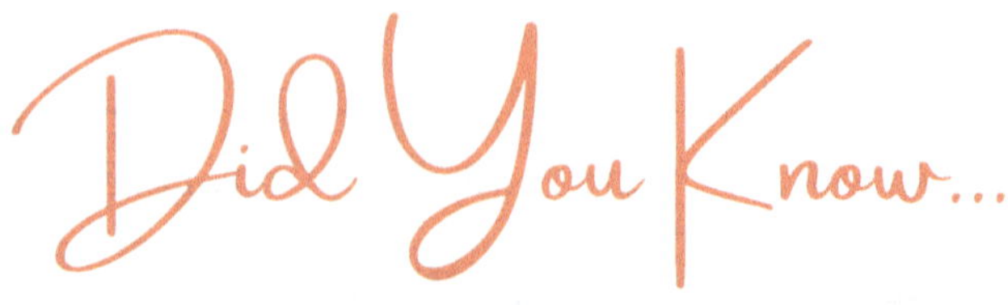

World's Fastest Speed on Towed Inline Skates

Holding onto a car while wearing inline skates to gain speed is an exhilarating and daring feat that many thrill-seekers have attempted over the years. However, it was Tobias Gustafsson who took this adrenaline-fueled activity to unprecedented heights in 2001. With nerves of steel and a determination to push the boundaries of speed skating, Gustafsson embarked on a record-breaking endeavor that would leave spectators in awe.

Clad in his inline skates and gripping onto the back of a speeding car, Gustafsson hurtled down the road with astonishing velocity. As the car accelerated, he held on tight, harnessing the vehicle's momentum to propel himself forward at breakneck speed. With each passing moment, Gustafsson's heart pounded in his chest as he raced against the wind, his eyes fixed on the horizon ahead.

In a breathtaking display of skill and bravery, Gustafsson shattered previous speed records, reaching an astonishing maximum speed of 262.7 kilometers per hour (163 miles per hour). The rush of adrenaline coursing through his veins was matched only by the sheer exhilaration of achieving such an incredible feat. With the wind whipping past him and the pavement blurring beneath his wheels, Gustafsson felt alive in a way he had never experienced before.

Gustafsson's remarkable achievement captured the imagination of speed skating enthusiasts around the world, cementing his legacy as a trailblazer in the sport. His daring pursuit of speed serves as a testament to the human spirit's relentless quest for adventure and exploration. And while his record-setting run may have been fleeting, the memory of his awe-inspiring feat continues to inspire future generations of thrill-seekers to chase their own dreams of adrenaline-fueled glory.

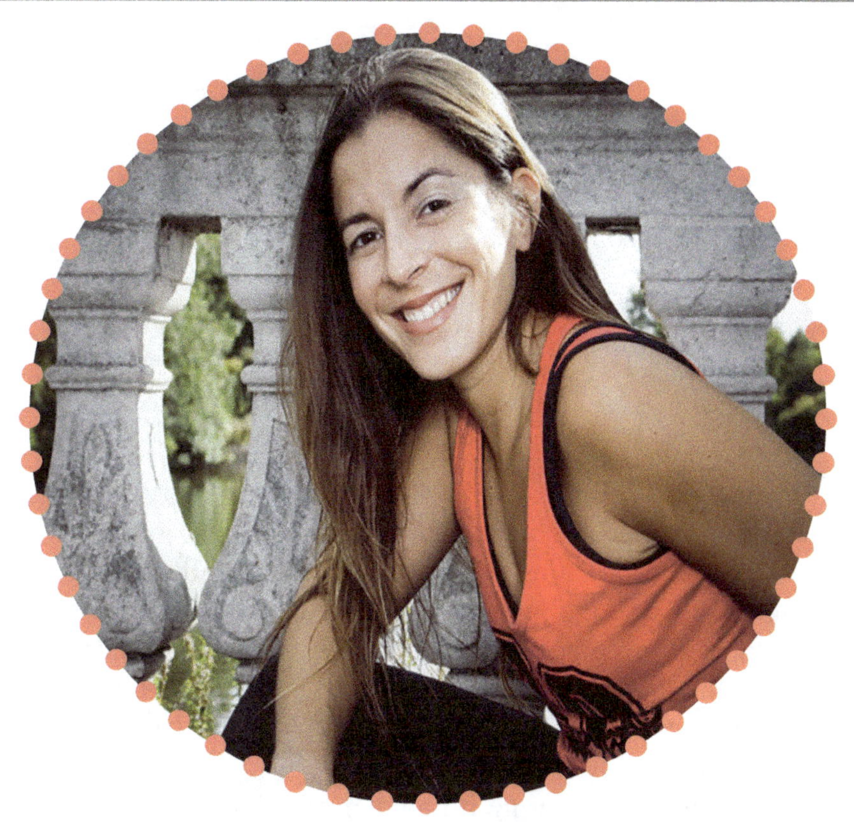

Delisa Garcia

Facebook: @Delisa Garcia | Instagram: @delisa_rollerdance

"The Two Sides of Me"

I am Spanish, born in the little coastal village of Puerto Sagunto in Valencia and this is where it all started…

I still remember skating with my first pair of roller skates six or seven years old. My first pair of roller skates were adjustable metal frames that had to be strapped to my shoes and a very hard set of wheels. Within a couple of years, they were upgraded to a beautiful pair of white leather boots. Little did I know back then what this would mean for me later in life!

In case you are wondering if I am a professional roller skater, the answer is no. I don't make a living out of roller skating, but I am not too bad at it, and during my time at university I had a few skating jobs. Professionally I have two masters one in Chemistry and a second one in Biomolecular Science, a PhD in Biophysics. Nowadays I work for a scientific German company called ZEISS as a head of software sales.

Back in the late eighties, roller skating was still a "thing." There was a small outdoor roller disco in my village, next to the beach, that was quite popular during - spring- and summer. I remember many Sunday afternoons my parents went out for a walk and rather than walk, I preferred to roller skate. I used to skate past the roller disco, wishing I was old enough to skate there. Unfortunately, it closed before I became old enough to go. Nowadays, that same place is an open-roof nightclub that opens during the summer. Roller skating faded and was just something only for "small kids." Nevertheless, I still enjoyed going for a stroll from time to time.

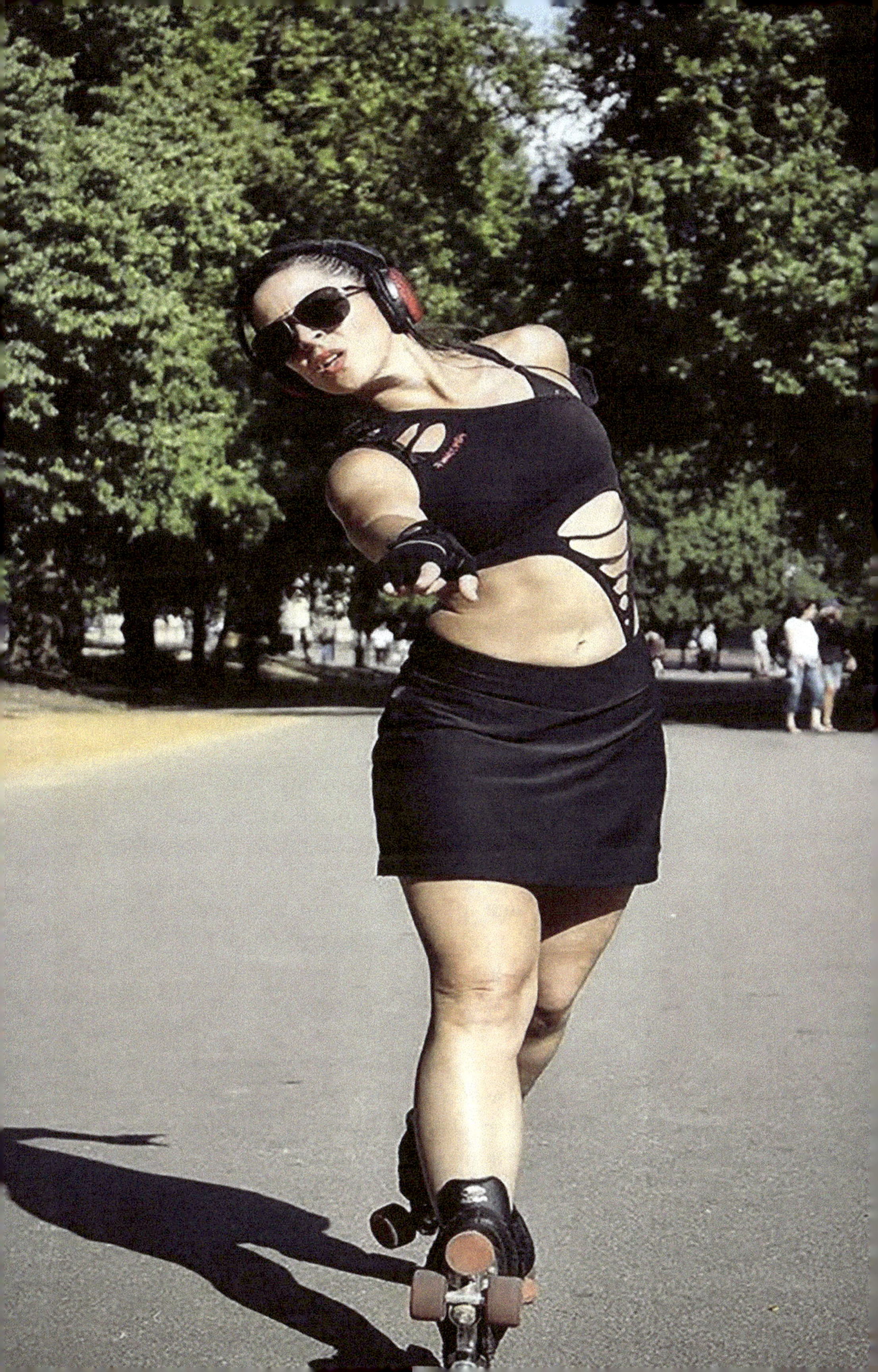

During my teens, inline skates became fashionable, and yes! Believe it or not, I ended up owning three different pairs of inline skates. I was always trying to convince my friends to go out skating and stroll around the village. At the time I knew nothing about roller dancing, doing cones with inlines, or any other type of skating modality.

I always enjoyed putting my skates on, but the craze for inline skating was short-lived (remember that I am still in my little village!) and skating was not the "cool" thing to do as a sixteen- or eighteen-year-old. So, the skates went back to the deep end of the closet.

I did a degree in organic chemistry in Valencia and I was offered the opportunity to be an Erasmus student. Back then, Erasmus was a European exchange student scheme via which a handful of students were given the opportunity to study for three to nine months at a different European university. This is how I ended up in London in September 2000 with a nine-month studentship to do the last year of my chemistry degree at Imperial College.

Back in those days, Sundays were a bit boring. My university friends went to visit or spent the day with their families or had too much to study. Hence, there was not much going on. I remember one day, walking through Hyde Park and spending some time watching a big group of roller skaters, dancing to the music coming from a stereo—jumping, spinning, sliding. Wow! I could watch them for hours!

I managed the courage to talk to one of them and ask where I could buy some roller skates. It looked like so much fun! They were dancing, which I always loved, and they were skating, which I also used to like back in the day. Best of all, they were dancing on quads, which brought me back to the old memories.

So, I went to Skate Attack and bought a new pair of roller skates. The next Sunday, there I was with my new skates. I suppose this is also how most people start skating, by watching other skaters that inspired them to try something new.

How difficult could it be to start skating again? Well, a bit! To be honest, that very first day that I put on the skates, it did not feel very good. I could not skate much, how did I used to do it back then?.

Nevertheless, it was fun, and I started appearing every single Sunday in Hyde Park with my new pair of roller skates.

I started to meet many new people: Dionne, Tyrone, Wayne, Selwyn, Golby, Seth, and Lisa. So many cool moves I wanted to do! So, the journey began. I was hooked straight away.

I learned my first steps from Tyrone; he had moves for every song and every beat, and Dionne. The first time I saw somebody doing the crazy legs move was Dionne. At the time I didn't even think it was called crazy legs. (Back then moves where moves and they did not have names like they have now). The move was so smooth and she looked so sexy while doing it!

Back in those days, we used to skate from Hyde Park to Trafalgar Square. Skating through the traffic on Piccadilly Road, buzzing through people at Piccadilly Circus, and then speeding down Haymarket. Wherever they were going, I was going! One of the first times, I remember Big Ness pulling me up Piccadilly Road (I was too slow). How could they skate so fast? I felt like flying!

I met Selwyn and Golby. Two of a kind with a very characteristic style. You can always recognize Selwyn skating in black and white and Golby skating in black and red.

"We are going to the Wednesday London skate. Come with us?" they said.

"Mmmm, I am not too sure. I just started skating a few weeks ago!"

"Don't worry," said Golby, "I will help you."

"Oh well, why not?"

I have managed to skate a few times from Hyde Park to Trafalgar Square (around one to one and a half miles). Surely, I can do a two-hour street skate (around ten to twelve miles long). What could go wrong? Well, down hill can go wrong when you do not know how to stop! Duh!

I felt too ashamed to ask somebody for help at the beginning of the downhill. I was kind of managing doing a T-stop, but there was a point where the speed was a bit too much and the T-stop was not working anymore for me and my abilities back then. So, there I was like a wild horse going down the hill, pushing people out of my way, trying to figure out how I was going to stop. Should I throw myself on the road? How can I fall to minimize the damage? Uh, oh, maybe I can just crash against everybody at the bottom of the hill… Oh gosh! And where is this guy that told me he was going to help me? F**k!

Just then, out of nowhere, a guy grabbed me, picked me up and, just like that, he carried me to the bottom of the hill. Wow! Just like Superman, but without a cape and with a pair of skates! No broken bones, no broken teeth… This guy really came to help me!

Believe it or not, this was the beginning of a love story, or love at a first roller skate. Since then, it has been over fifteen years together (I have lost count), a seven-year-old daughter and I am still trying to figure out how he saved me from that down hill.. Paul (aka Golby) is my Superman on skates, my "other skate" , because when I skate without him it feels like skating on one foot.Of course, since that day, I have not only found a partner but I've learned to stop in many ways!

What I like about skaters is that some of them have very specific looks or styles. Selwyn always dresses in black and white, Dionne has the hair and boxing boots converted to roller skates, Seth wears the hat and the white trousers, Wayne dances with the cane (and he is an icon in the London roller skating scene), and Lisa's skates are graffiti-painted. Therefore, I had to come up with my skating alter ego, too.

Red is a color that represents Spain in many ways (the passion, the Spanish flag, bull fights, flamenco…). Most of my favourite clothes are red, and instinctively I end up wearing all the time black and red sportwear with big leg warmers rolled over my skates when skating. Since Paul also wears black and red, we became the black and red skating couple.

The curious thing about creating a skating identity or skating style is that when people see you skating, they may not exactly remember you per se, but they will remember that they saw this person dressed in a certain way, doing something very amazing, and when the paths cross again, you get comments such as, "I saw you last year skating in xxx" or "I saw you in the xxx video" (when YouTube was just starting).

During the week, I am most of the time in front of the computer. Engaged in meetings, looking at market opportunities, doing scientific workshops, attending conferences. But during the weekend is play time! The computer is off and the skates are on! bye-bye smart business clothes and office, hello sportwear and outdoor spaces. People that has only meet me professionally can not believe what I do during the weekends. People that has met me while skating also finds surprising what I do professionally. The Yin and the Yang, Dr. Jekyll and Mr. Hyde, Dr. Garcia and Delisa roller dance. The two sides of me.

Skating is the highlight of the week. I am happy skating on my own or I can drop by Hyde Park and find some of the usual skaters to hang around with. When things go wrong or the stress at work is too much, I know skating will put a smile on my face. It will take the bad energy out and bring new positive energy in. Skating is a way to reconnect with my inner me, feel the air from the speed of my skates, and let myself go with the movement and rhythm of the music. Nothing else matters.

What I like about London skaters (and probably any other skating community in other countries) is that we have a huge variety of everything: cultural background, ethnicities, jobs, skating abilities, and ages. There are lawyers, engineers, nurses, vets, musicians, DJs, some work in a restaurant, others in a hotel or they are full-time professional roller skaters…anything goes. We are so different, but yet with something very strong that we all have in common: skating! This brings us together every Sunday, every week, and year after year.

Many years ago, we were all skating in Trafalgar Square when a blue-haired girl asked me if I could skate to one of her Michael Jackson's songs she had. She was from Barcelona on a tourist trip to London. She liked so much what we were doing that I could not say no to her, so I roller danced to her tune. Move forward five to eight years and I was on a business trip to Barcelona. My job takes me to many cities and different countries all around the world and wherever I go, I always take my skates in case I have a bit of free time to kill. On one of my trips to Barcelona, I connected with Michelle Barrios, the founder of Skate Love Barcelona and also a close friend of mine. During this trip, Michelle was telling me about how she had found a couple of other people interested in roller dancing and she introduced me to a red-haired girl on roller skates. After Michelle introduced us (she is Spanish but lives in London, blah, blah, blah) her eyes opened wide and lit. She said, "I met you many years ago during a trip to London in Trafalgar Square and that memory is what made me start skating when I met Michelle."

What are the chances of something like this happening? Just like that, she also became a very dear friend to me.

I love Barcelona! It does not have a regular roller disco or has the skating scene that London has, but for me, it is one of the best cities to skate outdoors and combine swimming in the sea, sunbathing and roller skating. I have met great people like Mireia, Michelle, Eddie, and Margot. I remember skating with Michelle on many occasions years before roller skating became what it is today in Barcelona, and experiencing for over ten years how she has grown—not only the skating scene in this city but also one of the best (at least for me) international skating events: SkateLove.

While skating is not my profession, it is the Yin to my Yang. During the weekdays, my life is very sedentary, spending many hours at my desk in front of the computer, dealing with many international projects and discussions on how to grow our scientific software business. But when the weekend comes, there is nothing better than roller skating in Hyde Park. Letting out the stress of work, skating for hours to compensate for the sedentary week, and enjoying the outdoors, the music, the dancing, and the people. There is no need to talk about work, no need to be solving problems or juggling hundreds of To-Do tasks. Skating connects me to the ground, and this instant moment is the only one that matters. I let the music feel me in and guide my movements while I skate. This makes me free, unwinds me from the week, recharges my batteries, allows me to see problems from a different perspective, and ultimately is my reset button.

Skating has also provided me with a social life outside of work and best of all, not only in London but also worldwide, like, for example, my lovely friend Kari Anne from Amsterdam. We've known each other now for over ten years! It is always so good when we have the chance to meet up during various skating events.

Skating also transformed my social lifestyle. Clubbing got replaced by roller discos, and outdoor festivals are mostly on skates, like the

Notting Hill Carnival. It is so much fun to do the carnival on roller skates!

One of the first, and only, roller discos in London when I started skating was Bagley's (later reopened as Canvas) in Kings Cross. I used to go there with many other skaters every week at least two times a week! It was an honor to have met Tony Askew, the owner of Bagley's roller disco. He was an extraordinary promoter of roller skating and always let us go in for free, something for which I will always be grateful. Years later, Canvas was relocated to Vauxhall (Renaissance Rooms), right on my doorstep. Renaissance Rooms closed in 2015 and a few years ago, it reopened in Tottenham as Roller Nation.

I enjoyed skating so much that I also started artistic skating and I enrolled in the London and Essex roller skating club in my late twenties. Completely different from roller dancing! I knew very well how to skate, but I was completely unaware of EDGES! I did solo dance for around eight years. During this time, I mastered edges (or at least tried to!) and learned some compulsory dances. I could not believe that all these compulsory dances had to be performed with some boring "organ with a beat" type of music. I never was a top skater compared to other people that had been doing artistic skating since they were small, but I still won some local competitions and even competed at the British Championships where I would always end up third or fourth—from the bottom!

Through skating, I also met my partner, my "other skate" and in 2016, Paul and I had a little daughter: Lucia. Our little ray of sunshine was born in England but with Spanish and Jamaican blood. Because of motherhood, I stopped artistic roller skating (not enough hours in a day for everything). But pregnancy did not mean that I was going to stop skating. I was five to six months pregnant and skating during Skate Love Barcelona 2015. I could not have missed it! During the 2015 Skate Love, I met Lotter who was also pregnant at the time., . I only really stopped skating during the last few weeks of pregnancy. This was a personal, beautiful experience on its own, but it also attracted all types of comments from unknown people—luckily mostly good, and for the not-so-good ones, I simply didn't care. When you skate, you learn about not caring about what other people think (especially people you don't know).

My daughter Lucia got her first pair of rollerskates at thirteen months old, just a few months after she learned how to walk. She is now seven years old, and she loves skating. One of her favorite things is roller discos (surprise, surprise!) and the Halloween London roller skate. She loves that the whole family and friends dress up and we all do the street skate. She has been doing this street skate for several years now (mostly pushed in her pram) and the last year she did the ten- to twelve-mile street skate on her own! She loves to do skating chains when we are in Hyde Park and she learned from the best (her daddy) to wind up the chain with sharp turns to see if the last person can hold on tight enough or if he or she gets a whip.

Now we are no longer the black and red couple, but the black and red family. I hope this little hobby grows in Lucia in the same way it has grown in us and brings her the same or more happiness in her life.

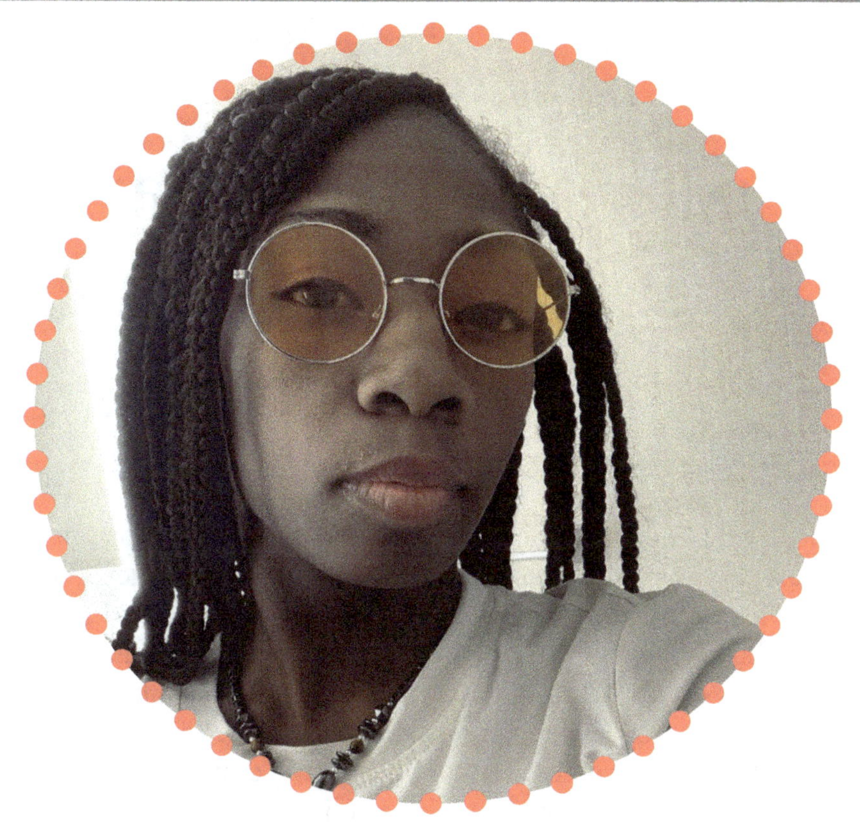

Keira Bell

aka Keke

Facebook: @Keira Gilliam | Instagram: @keketoldmedat

"My Forever Boyfriend"

Those who know me know I love, love, love to skate fast, but that wasn't always the case. I started skating at the age of seven. My parents dropped me off at the Albion Skating Rink with all my neighborhood friends. I knew nothing about skating; I was sitting on the sidelines until I heard my favorite Mariah Carey song and I said, "Oooowee, I'm gonna skate to this song." I scooted from one end of the floor to the other. After that point, I knew skating was for me. It was just the feeling I had when I stepped on the floor and moved on the wood. Even in my infantile state, I knew it was for me. I skated every weekend until this rink closed. There weren't a lot of other places to skate, so skating faded off for me.

I started college at Michigan State and went to a skate party, where I rekindled my love affair with skating. I went to the regular skate parties until I started attending the adult skating session on Sunday nights. I was in awe. The music, the moves, and the atmosphere had me on cloud nine. As I watched the floor, there was this one dude, who was kicking and spinning and kick-spinning and I said, "I want to be just like him." That man is Joe Carter, and he is my idol to this day. This inspired me to get my own skates and get deeper into the culture.

Skating has saved my life on multiple occasions. I am so grateful for being able to turn to skating. As I battled anxiety, depression, and grief, I turned to the rink. I am not sure what I would have done without it. I love to eat. People wouldn't know this about me because

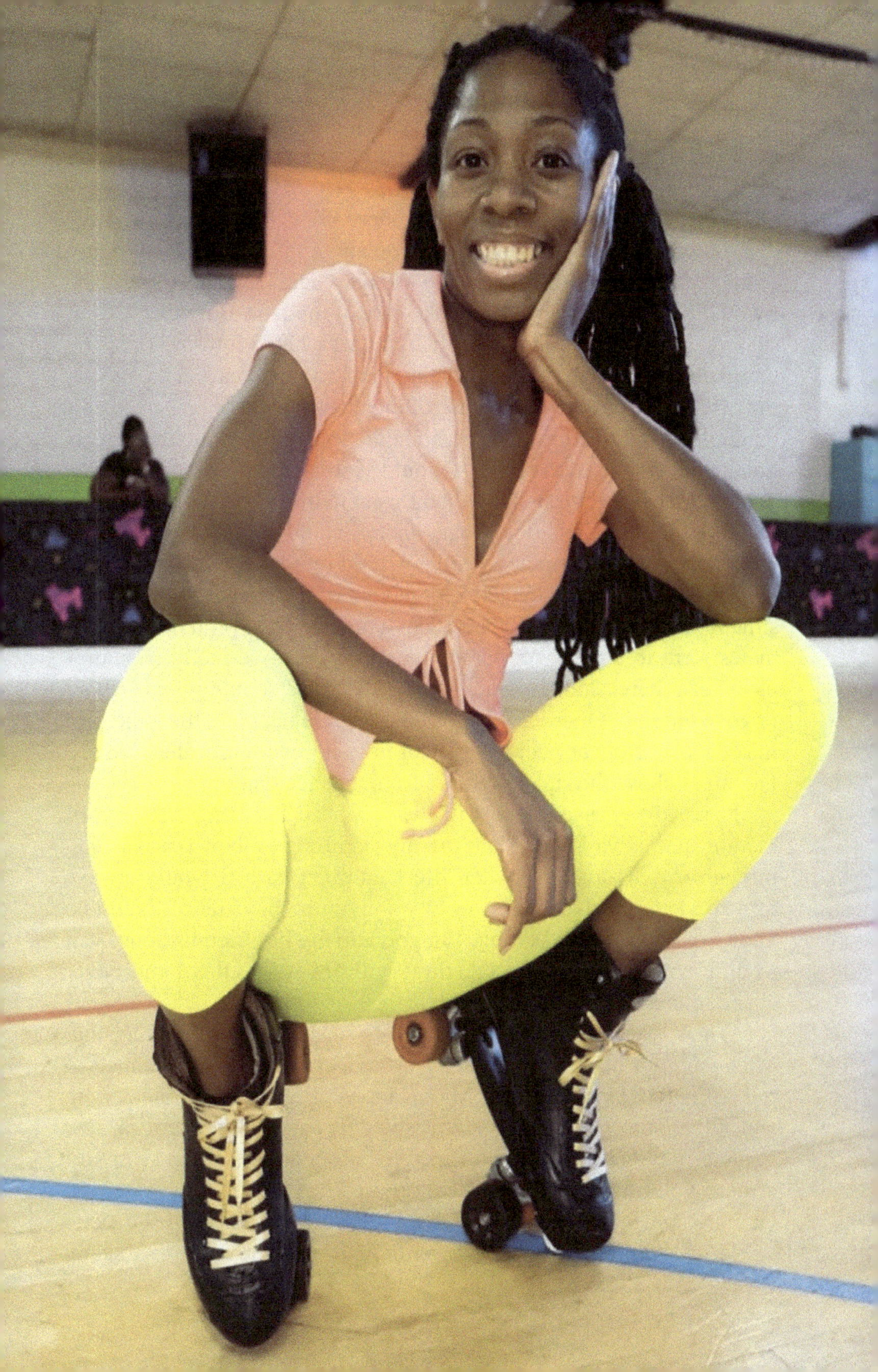

of my small stature, but I can eat and eat a lot. But I roll so hard, skating keeps me in shape.

College was very stressful and there were times I would have depressive episodes where I couldn't do anything. I mean I was really doing the bare minimum to survive when I would have these episodes. I would barely wash myself, or take care of my hair. But when I went skating, my entire being changed. When I walked into the rink, my world changed. That feeling of being inside a rink, hearing the music, the people, the environment, and rolling on the wood floor—that can't be duplicated. Skating became an addiction. When something feels good, you want it all the time. I would skate in my dorm room or any random place to get it in, but when I went to the rink, I let it all out on the floor. On the flip side of that, when I would put on my coat to go home, that lost and hopeless feeling would return.

Skating saved my life and kept me out of questionable and unsafe situations more than once. There was a time when several of my dorm mates went to a party off campus. Let me say—we really shouldn't have been there. I struggled with myself on if I should go with them or go to the rink. Of course, I chose the latter. That night the ladies got into a really bad car accident. Thankfully no one was killed, but the fact that I chose the rink saved me from that accident.

I have always used skating to clear my head and bring me comfort. Skating has always been one of my comforts. When I was going through my divorce and when life would get hard, I would always turn to skating. I call skating my long-term boyfriend. Everyone knows that when I go skating, I'm going to my boyfriend's house just in different places, but he (skating) will always be there and never abandon me, nor I him.

When I left college, I continued to skate. I stayed in Lansing, Michigan, got married and attended the local rink, and continued to roll at EDRU Skate in Holt, Michigan. At EDRU, the skaters were and still are more seasoned, so I wasn't able to see all the "tricks" and varying moves and styles, so I traveled around the state in search of a more youthful and diverse skating crowd. I visited Flint, Detroit, Grand Rapids, and Big Parker. I wanted to experience all the skate world had to offer. Skating is my life. My ex-husband didn't skate, and it was a problem, but he let me be. Although he knew I loved skating, as that was my world when we met, he had reservations about me being at a rink, skating until 4:00 a.m. He tried to skate, but it was never his thing. I would invite him to watch other people's Facebook or Instagram live to verify that the party was going on until this time and I was there but eventually, it (my love for my skating and intensity) became too much for him to bear, thus we divorced.

Over the years, skating culture has changed drastically. At my rink, I am one of the younger people in the rink, but when I go abroad, I become the old skater. The age and style of the younger skaters stress me out a little because I don't think it's about the music as it is about the moves. We're doing some really fancy spins and things. Don't get me wrong, the moves are amazing, but it's no longer about the music. They are no longer skating to the music. They are just doing what they do, no longer fitting to the music. This is stressful for me to see. I don't want the culture to go that way where we lose the music. Music has always been a part of what we do in every region of the country. Music has influenced how we skate. When I came up in college, skating to a slow song meant finding a partner to skate slow, and on beat. Now when a slow song comes on, skaters just continue to skate full speed ahead, not changing the pace one bit.

The music in Detroit is traditionally old-school music, which is where the styles originated. Back in the day, we listened to this same music in our cars, clubs and, of course, in the rink—that was our music. New skaters seem not to have this same connection to the music. In other places like Grand Rapids, they play trap music and other things they feel Black skaters listen to.

After all these years, the one thing that makes me smile when I think about skating is the music that's played. When you are there and your jam comes on, that's it! 'Cause if it's my jam and I hear it, I lose my mind—that go-to song for me is "Blow the Whistle" by Too Short, and yep, it's an old tune and yep, I get tired of it, but if I don't hear it in the rink, I get an attitude. That song is my fire. When I hear this jam, I can be in mid-conversation with someone, and my ears perk up. I pop out of my seat and hit the floor and skate really, really fast. That's how I skate—faster than most around the rink. At our rink, there really isn't any style, so I just skate fast and get lost in the beat. When "Blow the Whistle" comes on when I'm rolling in Northland Rink, I lose my mind. This rink is so big and the floor is smooth.

After all these years, I don't have the desire to stop skating, but I feel like I need to change my surrounding, i.e., maybe choosing to skate in different locations outside of the rink. I'm that person who enters the rink, put on my skates and I am on the floor all night. Know at a national party, if I arrive at midnight, I will be skating until six am or until that rink close. Skating is serious exercise for me. I have never been a runner, but rolling on these 8s, I can do six miles with ease. I do a little middle work, but for the most part, I'll be the one on the outside rolling at the speed of light.

Along my skate journey, so many people have inspired me along the way. Richard Manning, the way he skates, and his energy and fearlessness on the floor are inspiring. Angie McClendon and Lisa McFadden skate like they are one with the music. This makes my heart smile. So many skaters along the way have inspired me—I cannot name them all.

Skate parties nowadays are plentiful and make it hard to choose which one to attend, so I choose places I haven't gone to before. I'm always looking for something new to explore. Lately, I have met a few people that I have seen on TV shows and/or commercials and I find this is a great feeling when I meet them in person. I would also love to be involved with being on a commercial/TV show, so if yall are looking, I'm here.

It was, and still is, interesting how people see me skating and they ask, "Do people still skate?" Our culture never stopped skating. When I skate outside, I do trail skating. I am looking to create a group of Trail Skating here in Michigan. I experienced this in Chicago when attending IR and I love it and want to bring that to my hometown.

Skating can change your life. Skating is fun and you don't realize all the benefits of skating and so many things you can do with skating. I want to impart to the readers: I want us all to be encouraged. While I know we have our own struggles, issues, and politics, stay strong, continue to skate, and continue to uplift the culture. Continue to push forward and persevere...

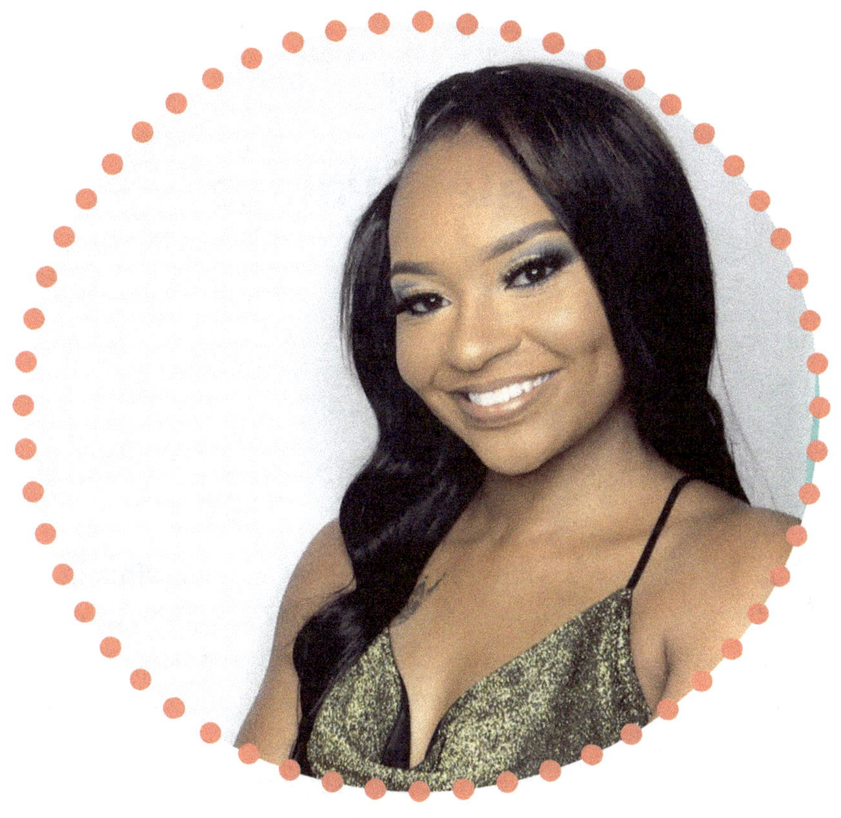

Tyeila Kimiara Gant

aka Royãl

Facebook: @Royãle Gant | Instagram: @royal_gant

“Royãle’s Palace”

When I fell in love with skating, it all began with spinning. At the start of my skating journey, I was eager to explore every skate style, and I did just that. However, mastering the art of spinning quickly became my favorite pursuit. There’s something incredibly fulfilling about the spiritual connection you can achieve while spinning in your roller skates. The harmony between the strength of your core and the pressure on the balls of your feet is truly special. For me, spinning is not just a physical activity; it’s a way of expressing myself spiritually. I find that connecting to the music elevates spinning to a whole new level of spiritual experience.

People often ask me, “How do you avoid getting dizzy when you spin, Royãle?” My answer is always the same: “Connecting to the music is the key to preventing dizziness. Once you experience it, you’ll understand the feeling, and you won’t want to stop spinning.”

My passion for spinning is so strong that I aspire to teach it to people of all ages. There are countless ways to spin – on your toes, with all wheels, bending down, fast or slow – each offering a unique form of self-expression. What’s most captivating about spinning is that it’s all about feeling and movement, without the need for facial expressions.

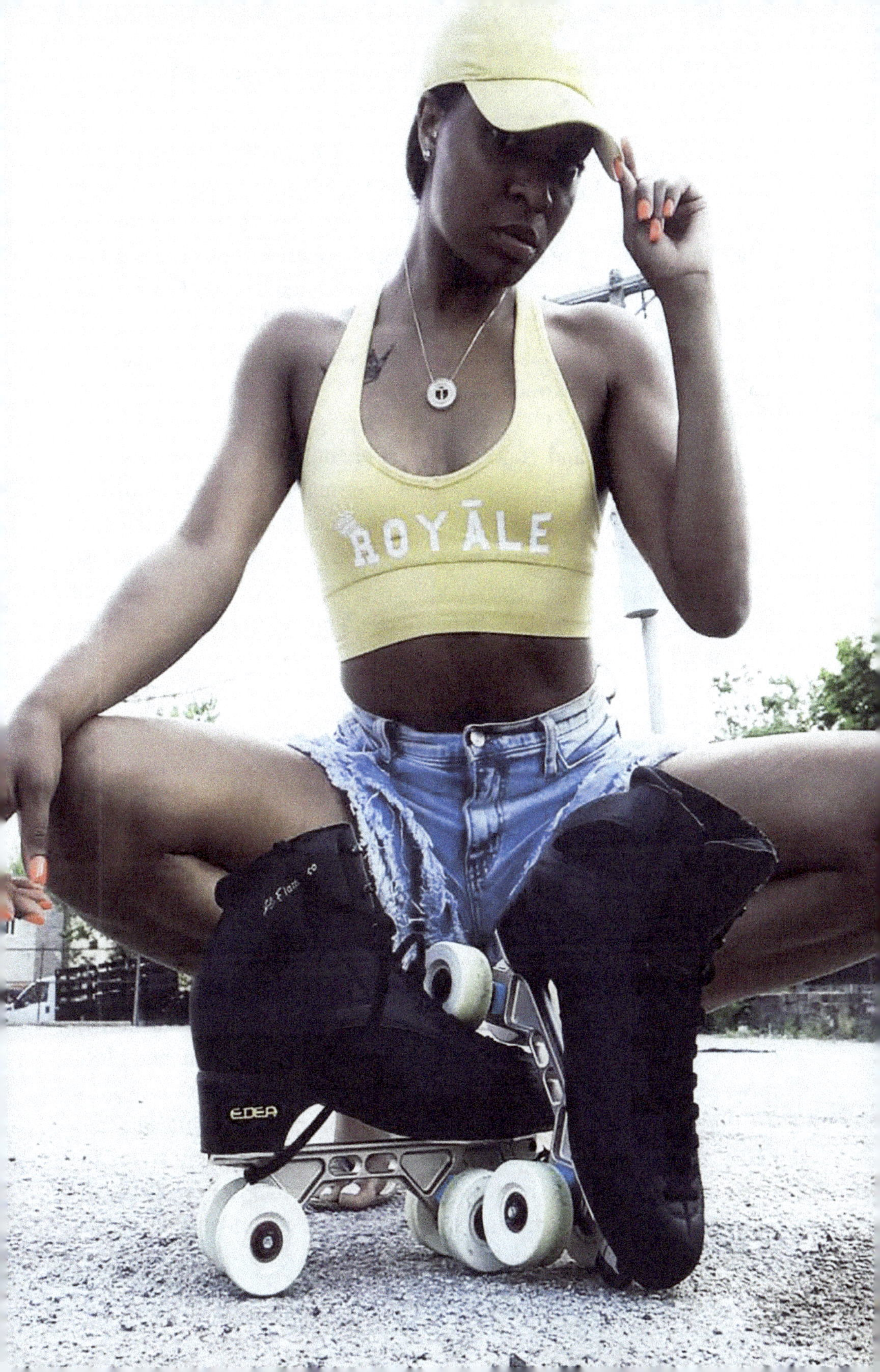
ROYĀLE
EDEA

Roller skating holds a special place in my heart; it's like the rhythm to my heartbeat. I love immersing myself in a song and enjoying every moment of it while skating. My favorite song to spin to is "Tell Me" by Usher, but I also enjoy skating to R&B, alternative, rock, and hip-hop music. I want to give a big shout-out to our skater DJs: DJ Bounce, DJ Problem Child, DJ Wild Child, and DJ Bowen. Watching them grow over the years has been inspiring, and they keep me motivated to treat skating as both a workout and a sport.

Skating with my OG's is always a smooth experience. I love the graceful edges and curves you can create with your wheels. The camaraderie and energy in the skate community are truly uplifting. Many people have inspired me to keep shining my light, including Myesha the SmoothGoddess, Sean-Christopher, Cece-the Realest, and Bad Boys Crew. Skaters and DJs alike motivate me with their hard work and passion. Together, we teach ourselves, each other, and those in our community.

Our skate community is diverse and inclusive, welcoming people of all ages and backgrounds. It's a place where you can truly be yourself and express your individuality. I started skating at twenty-six, and I've learned that as long as I keep loving what I do and practicing, I can achieve my goals and aspirations. I'm excited to see where my skate journey will take me in the future, including starting a family and teaching my future kids how to skate.

Recently, I've taken up filming skaters to capture their moments on camera. It's important for skaters to have footage for their resumes and future opportunities. I enjoy capturing skaters in their element, especially when the lighting is just right and they're glowing in their moves. Outfits also play a big part in capturing the moment, and I look forward to supporting skaters in promoting their style of skating.

Filming skaters is exciting because it feels like capturing a concert or dancers on skates. Skaters have created so many different styles and ways to skate together, inspiring all ages of skaters to become better. I also enjoy capturing the energy of youth skaters under twelve, who bring a fresh perspective and motivation to the skate community.

In addition to filming, I'm excited to teach youth how to skate and pave the way for future generations of skaters. I've always had a passion for skating and dancing, which I started at four years old. Dancing translated into ice and roller skating, becoming another way for me to express myself. Dancing brings a sense of self-love and allows you to communicate how you feel without using words.

Performing on stage is another way I express myself, and I look forward to those moments when the lights come on and the crowd's energy is palpable. Competing has been a part of my life since I was four years old, instilling in me a love for sports and staying active. Supporting the community is important to me, as we rely on each other for healing, love, and motivation. Skaters support each other through hard times and celebrate together during the good times.

I've appreciated the love and support I've received throughout my skate journey, and I'm excited for the next chapter in life. I know it will include skating and starting a family, and I'm grateful for the opportunity to support future generations of skaters. Finally, I want to thank my support system for pushing me to be greater every day, and I look forward to connecting with others who share my passion for skating and spreading positive energy.

Did You Know...

Roller Skating vs. Skateboarding

Roller skating and skateboarding are both popular recreational activities that involve riding on wheels, but they differ in several key aspects. Roller skating typically involves wearing roller skates with wheels arranged in a rectangular configuration or inline skates with wheels in a straight line, allowing for smooth movement on solid ground. In contrast, skateboarding utilizes a single board with wheels, known as a skateboard, which is propelled by pushing off with one foot and balancing on the board. The techniques and maneuvers used in roller skating and skateboarding vary significantly due to differences in equipment and riding styles. Roller skaters often perform graceful movements and spins, utilizing the stability provided by the wheels and the ability to glide smoothly across surfaces. Skateboarders, on the other hand, execute tricks and maneuvers such as ollies, kickflips, and grinds, utilizing the agility and maneuverability of the skateboard to navigate obstacles and terrain. Additionally, while roller skating can be done indoors or outdoors on smooth surfaces, skateboarding is often associated with urban environments, skate parks, and street skating, where skateboarders utilize ramps, rails, and other features to perform tricks. Despite these differences, both roller skating and skateboarding offer exhilarating experiences and opportunities for self-expression and creativity.

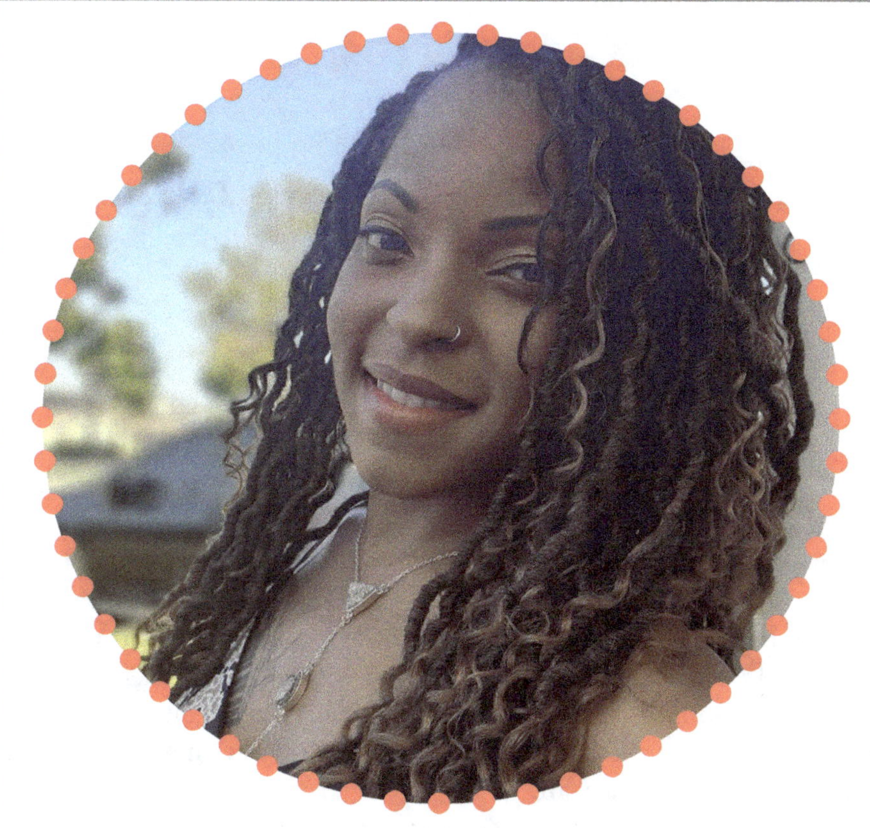

Chaz M. Cunningham Coggins

aka DJ Lady P

Facebook: @dj Lady P | Instagram: @djladyp

"Butterfly Season: The Birth of Lady P"

Formally known as Miss CC-Lady Poetess, now known as DJ Lady P—I was born in Long Beach, CA. Primarily raised in the Inland Empire Region with my Mom, I spent the rest of my time in West LA with my Dad. At the young age of nine years old, I went from being a fully functional outgoing athlete physically and a quick learner in general—to a girl whose life turned upside down with a sudden brain hemorrhage and aneurysm.

Following two brain surgeries in 1995, plus a third unsuccessful surgery—I endured two strokes leaving me with a physical disability on the left side. These events also left me with a learning disability from having a portion of my brain removed. Starting completely over, I had to re-learn everything from the basics and everything else going forward. It came with challenges I never imagined, including learning who I was as a person all over again. However, in losing part of my brain functionality—my artistic side became more enhanced. Later on, in 2018, I decided after receiving unexpected news to have my final brain surgery.

At the time during my marriage, I desired to have children—which would also require me to have brain surgery. The result would be starting over with a different set of challenges. Nonetheless, it would be a beautiful discovery of self—in my own ugly but also amazing way—as I put it. Unfortunately, I did not have the support of my spouse and decided to divorce from an unhealthy environment during the process.

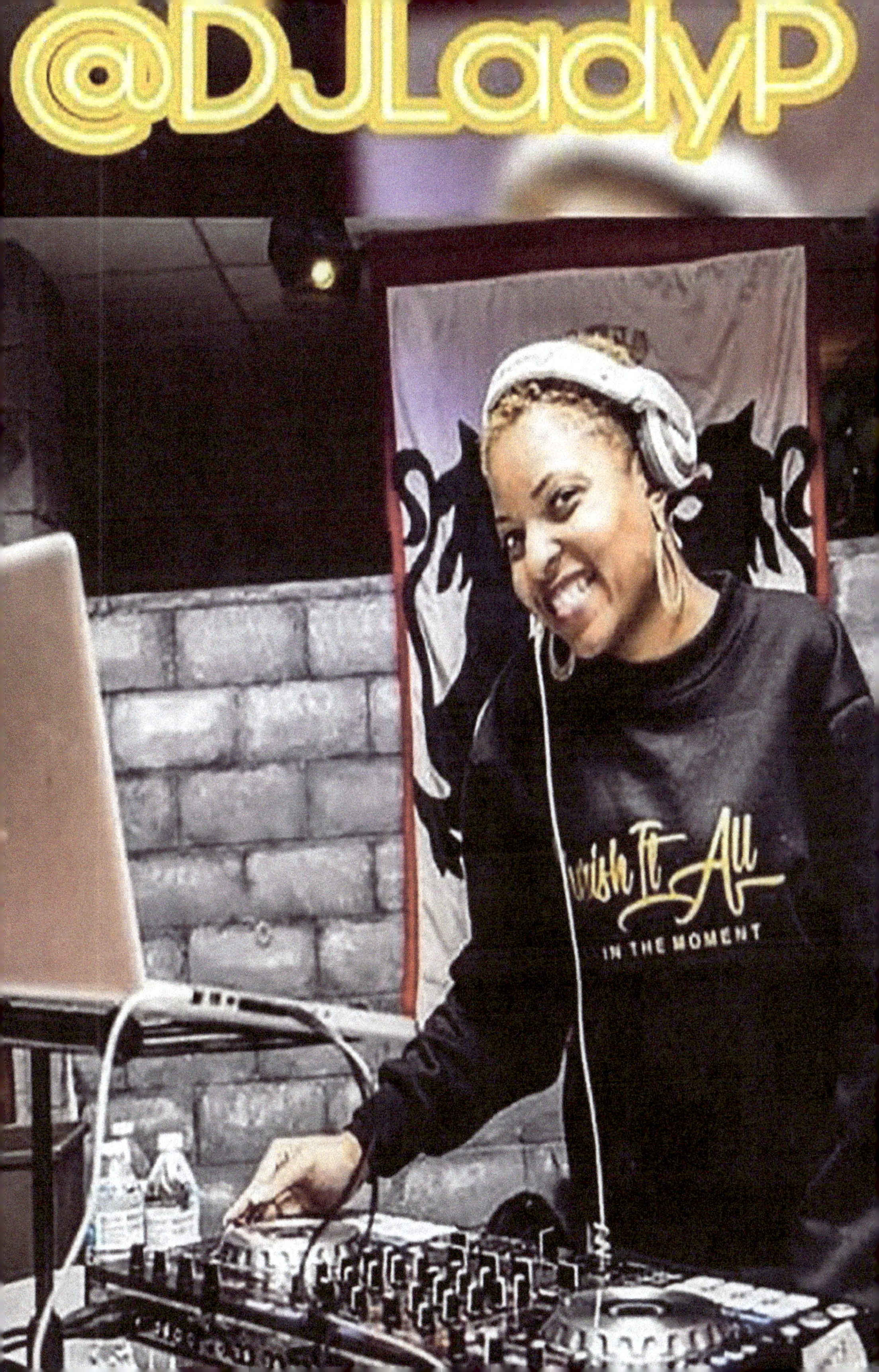
@DJLadyP
IN THE MOMENT

I developed a love for music and poetry overall in Elementary School. Making my mark as a poet in college, I created the name Miss CC-Lady Poetess to stand for the elegance of a 'Lady.' Keeping my initials, a friend gave me the name 'Lady P' when I transitioned into being a DJ. Interestingly, I initially went to college to become a chef, majoring in culinary arts but keeping up started to become both physically and mentally challenging; dealing with subtle discrimination in workplaces from having a disability was stunting my ability to get the career I originally desired. However, my love for the arts, music, and anything dealing with expression or audio grew—as it was my way of coping with life challenges.

By age twenty-six, DJ Lady P (me) decided to invest in the dream of becoming a Professional DJ determined to fulfill my purpose and passion. As one of the first female Radio DJs with Beyond the Mic Radio Show on Urban Soul Radio—I made a mark. Making DJ appearances at Soulful Sessions with my former artistic family Jouissance of Expression, So. Cal's Natural Beauty Pageant for Flourishe, RawArtists Pomona Showcase, Da Poetry, and Music Lounge, Xpressions with Holla At Ya Boy Entertainment, Accelerated Radio, All Rhythm Radio, Secret Society Sundays at Nola's with GiftJoy Entertainment, Lemon Flavor Boutique Fashion Show, G&C Media Ent. Events, Rock Boy Fresh Unplugged Concert, The International DJ Cafe, Platinum DJ Cafe, Fireproof the stage play, The Music & Poetry Lounge at The Hilton Hotel, Warrior Women Community, Skate Express, Euphony Restaurant and Lounge, Sevilla's Restaurant, also traveling out of town for other special events, parties, Skate Parties such as ATL's Old School Skate Jam w/ The Super Family, State2State, Sk8fanatics Cali Slide, Skate Lisa's Events, Venice Beach Rollers, East Meets West, Ajaxx, The Sk8Popup, Dallas Sk8 Fair Classic, True Skater Weekend and more. I had the honor of deejaying for some amazing artists— both unsigned and Grammy Award-winning and most importantly community-driven events to give back with the most recent being for the NAACP Pasadena Chapter for their 'Rally for Black Lives.' Specializing in spinning various genres of music works for me, but my favorite type of music to jam to is R&B, 90's, and Old School. I was a DJ on 94.5 The Blaze, Street Madness Radio in Atlanta, and I currently deejay and intern at IMG Radio Network.

Presently traveling all over the country and declared the First Lady of The Platinum DJ Team; as well as MP Productions. You can always expect a personable interaction when working with me; as I am anxious to keep people moving to 'Feel Good Music.'

The quote I use to motivate myself and others in the field of deejaying is that

"Music is the sound of Emotion."

Difficulties have shown their face throughout my journey—as such it has been difficult as a Black disabled woman in a male-dominated field, however, it's also been a strengthening and humbling learning experience. It's also made me fight harder for many others like myself and those that are worse off.

You tend to face discrimination at times because of ethnicity, gender, disability, and the more I say this—the better. "It's important to keep going while remembering your purpose through it all."

I believe it's been important to rely on Faith and the tools God has given me to make whatever positive impact we can on the community and the world.

My first experience coming into the skate world stemmed from going to the skating rink with my sister on Friday nights at Skate Express in Chino, Ca. I enjoyed watching everyone and had never really taken in a skate experience like that before outside of getting your regular pair of skates and going outside as a child. It was a different world. Seeing routines, couples skating, tricks—was therapeutic for so many. I wanted to try it, but was timid at first. Especially since spotting this guy who I thought was cute—and didn't want to embarrass myself in front of him knowing my physical limitations. Funny thing is, later on in the night—he approached me as he had been subtly watching my moves. He convinced me to try on some skates and wanted to take me out on the floor. Nervous like a little girl with a schoolboy crush, we did just that—and skated most of the night together, with me getting his number afterward.

I not only fell even more in love with skating but also fell in love with my first boyfriend, as well as my first love. I continued to go to the rink with my sister and meeting up with my boyfriend, and eventually invested in my first pair of skates. Being a tomboy at heart I got personal customs on a pair of skateboard Vans shoes. It was a lot of fun learning and getting out there when I could join the crowd. Primarily the nights that we went were Old School Nights and everyone was friendly, patient, and would look out for me on the floor so I didn't get hurt. At the time DJ Rodney Brewer was the DJ and it was like a family reunion as everyone either knew each other or were related. Chino became home for me. As time progressed, although I enjoyed skating, I felt slightly odd because I could only do so much. However, my love of music coupled with having a good ear; led to hoping that one day I could be a part of that world by deejaying—since I couldn't necessarily do all the routines and tricks. Ironically, I ended up doing just that—and the rest was history.

I started out doing family sessions after having a conversation with Scooby who was the DJ for the Hip Hop night at Skate Express during that time. I applied and had an interview with Joy who gave me a shot as a DJ employee. At first, it was boring for me because I didn't like playing pop and kids' music all day. But I knew I had to start somewhere. So, I did just that and would come up with ideas to present to Jerry the owner when the time was right. Eventually, I earned the ability to have my first adult session; I was incredibly nervous but sitting with my sister Brishae going over song ideas, learning the ins and outs of specials, and talking with close friends turned family—Meghan and Niya—getting their feedback as well, which was key. Learning as much as I could and adding flavor to it, I evolved into the DJ I am now in the skate world by not being afraid to step outside the box, try new things, introduce songs that hadn't gotten airplay before while also giving them music they were familiar with. Initially, it wasn't the most accepted as my approach was different.

Creatively I found a groove and before I knew it, I had unknowingly created a buzz and people began wondering who was this Lady P? My namesake's moniker started getting skaters visiting from other cities—without me knowing until it came to my attention. A solid recommendation by Pete of Skate Fanatics—led to my invitation to DJ the first out-of-town Skate Party in Northern California with 2Raw Skate. With excitement and nerves about the opportunity—I didn't have the best first experience facing challenges I wasn't prepared for. That was my first introduction to regional styles and the history of skate culture. From that point on— I committed to learn as much as I could worldwide—so that when another opportunity came, I would be ready.

Over time with much work put in the skate scene, I became the first West Coast female DJ to deejay in Atlanta, Texas, Arizona, and in 2019 an invitation to be on the itinerary for Soul Skate in Detroit rounded out a big year. Unfortunately, due to the pandemic hitting in 2020, Soul Skate got postponed. However, the humble honor of being a consideration serves as an accomplishment I can always cherish. Skating has developed my persona, Lady P—as a whole—because it teaches you to not only specialize in what you do musically, but as an individual to study, learn, and adapt to everything you encounter. That includes age demographic, regional styles of skating and music, the different cadences and beats that women and men skate to, the history behind tradition, art, DJs that paved the way, and the history of different rinks. Also included is how skating's pivotal role in ending segregation came about—and so much more. Unfortunately, there are skate politics that tend to unfold which can cause discord, competition, and at times can make things discouraging or stressful if you let it. Some of the challenges being a female DJ alone—have their grievances. However, not everyone plays into those things, which has been the good part. In which case I can focus on growing in my gift to be able to share and give back to our community because ultimately skating is therapy for many worldwide. Preserving that safe space is what truly matters most.

I have earned the title of a Professional Traveling DJ specializing in a variety of music. I'm also very big on being a community advocate and activist. In college, I created a group that specialized in all art forms: poetry, singing, musicianship, comedy, rapping, and more. A friend of mine named Michael had a clothing line called, Jouissance of Expression.

I asked Mike what it meant in their poetry class they were talking and he said it meant "Love of Expression" in French.

I told Michael about the idea for creating this group and asked about him incorporating the name of his clothing line with the group I wanted to start—he loved that idea. I then got things going creating flyers and driving around the city to get people to come to their first gathering at my house. Unfortunately, the first time only myself and three classmates showed up. We felt down, but not defeated, so I shared the idea with more students and people on campus. In the second meeting, we had six people, which for all of us—was an encouragement to keep trying. We soon expanded to twelve people, than twenty people and I also wanted to bring art to the youth and community.

So, we started reaching out to schools and group homes to help inner-city youth find their healing and escape through art while also giving back to the less fortunate. It became everyone's way of staying positive, healing, and paying it forward. Mike eventually turned the name and carrying out "Jouissance of Expression" to me, promising him to do right by the name. The group grew and flourished with team members, Vice President, and other roles for about five years closing out with a successful open mic night and jam session called "Soulful Sessions" in Rialto, Ca. Jouissance of Expression had come to an end as people moved, had families, and didn't have as much time to commit. However, so many good things happened— that it left a legacy and impact of its own.

Giving my own time to various community advocate causes—as my parents were also activists—led to my following in their footsteps. In my mind, what's the point of doing anything if it isn't for a purpose and it doesn't give back to the community? We all need a village and it's important to utilize our gifts for the greater good. Art as a whole provides healing, unity, a message, and so much more. I use this platform to create a change while accomplishing all of those things. I always take pride in telling a story through art that can deliver that. I do not believe in competition. Instead, I believe we each have a role to play in using our gifts and calling to change the world.

My favorite memory from childhood that I can remember would be learning music and writing from my musically inclined brother and cousin. They were my inspiration and who I looked up to. When 'Lady P' can't get out there to skate with people—you'll catch me enjoying an occasional piggyback ride from one of my skaters to join in on the fun. This exemplifies my love and passion for skating and all it has meant to my life!

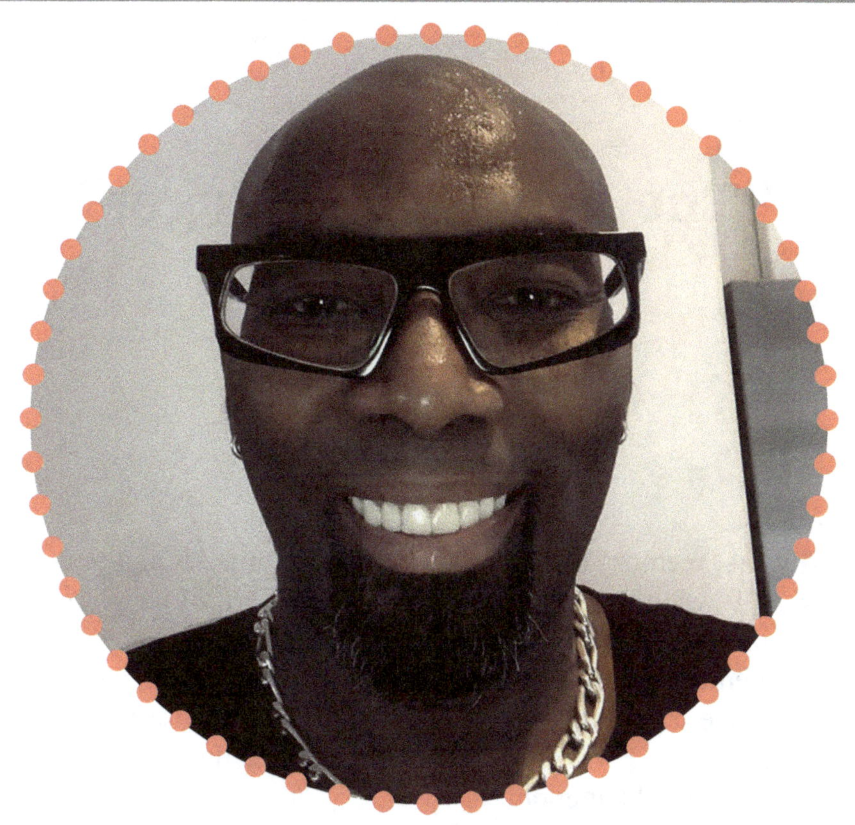

Tony Williams

aka Tyger

Facebook: @Tygar Skates | Instagram: @tigerwilliams8

"The Journey of a Tyger"

My first memory of roller skating in the United Kingdom was in 1979 when I was about seventeen years old. I caught sight of kids whizzing past me with wheels attached to Lonsdale boxing boots. The excitement spread like wildfire, and I was determined to join the skating craze. I couldn't afford a pair of skates because I was from a family of seven. I was the middle of seven and the firstborn of four here in the United Kingdom.

I vividly remember some of my friends with skates and I wanted some, so I began constructing my own pair of skates using old blue plastic rental ice skates boots I acquired from an Ice rink (we won't say how). Man, those boots were blue plastic and ugly looking, but I removed the ice blades and used four skateboard trucks, which I fitted to a piece of wood and attached to the bottom of the boots, and miraculously they stayed. I was soon skating up and down the neighborhood and in the streets for hours on end. I skated up and down the road and hills. This was the start of my love of skating. I jumped in them and went backward; in those days, it was all about going backward and side surfing (spread eagle) and area challenges to see who was the fastest at going backward. I was from Harlesden, North London, and we challenged kids in other areas like Kensal Rise, Chalk Hill Estate, and Stonebridge Estate. Good clean fun, those were the days. Now that I was gaining style and street cred, I had to have a

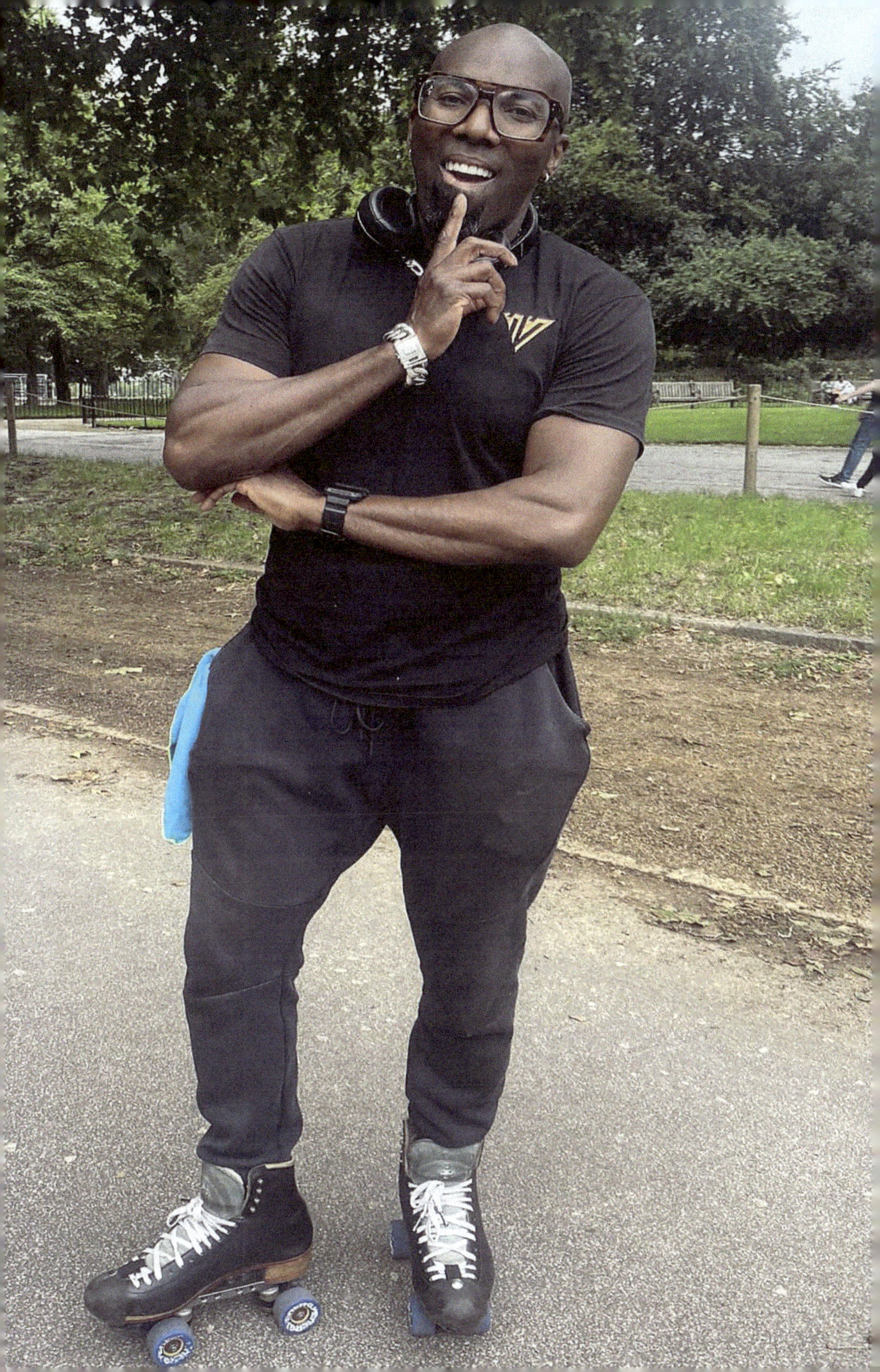

name to fit. I was born in 1962, which was the year of the Tiger in the Chinese New Year, so I chose "Tyger" as my skate name.

My parents were exasperated at my neglect of homework, but my passion for skating was all that mattered to me. Rain or cold, I would skate for miles, honing my skills in tricks and speed skating backward, and I always took along my big ghetto blaster (boombox). There were only a handful of roller discos in and around my area, which was Sk8citylondon, Starlight, and Byron Hall Harrow, which started back in the 1980s. I would go skating every Friday. We would also skate in Hammersmith, West London. Skaters also converged on Battersea Park, but the Council (UK Government) back in those days didn't like skaters, so they covered the skate area with lumps of tarmac to prevent us from skating there. Hyde Park was the next big spot where we assembled on and is still home for skaters today.

Fast forward to the present, and I'm still skating with the same enthusiasm. I founded a Facebook group called London Hyde Park Skaters in 2010, which has since amassed over four thousand members. While my skating style has evolved to incorporate more slow jams and free-style dancing, I'm delighted to see that my middle son, now thirty-two, also shares my love for skating. It's truly heartwarming to witness the younger generation embracing this art/sport and taking it to new heights.

As I approach my sixty-first year, I can proudly say that I'm still gliding along on my wheels with slow jams playing through my headphones. I was never one to follow routines. I was always a freestyler. When I skate, I make up my dance moves up on the spot when I feel the vibes. While the skating scene has changed over the years, with new equipment and styles emerging, the core passion for skating remains the same. It's a feeling of freedom and flow, of pushing oneself to new limits and experiencing the world in a unique way. I'm grateful for the memories and friendships that skating has brought into my life, and I look forward to many more years of gliding along on my trusty skates. Whether it's in Hyde Park or any other spot around the world, I know that there will always be a community of skaters ready to welcome me with open arms.

Beyond the physical joy of skating, it has also been a source of mental and emotional well-being for me. There's something about the rhythmic motion of skating that soothes the mind and lifts the spirit. It's a way to disconnect from the stresses of daily life and connect with oneself and the world around us. And the sense of community that comes with skating is truly special. From the early days of skating on the streets to the organized events and meet-ups of today, there's a bond that forms between skaters that transcend age, race, and background. It's a shared passion that brings people together and creates lifelong friendships. So, as I continue to skate into my golden years, I'm grateful for all that this sport has given me and excited to see where it will take me next.

Did You Know...

Getting Married on Skates?

The first recorded marriage on roller skates is a charming and unconventional tale that took place in 1912, setting a precedent for unique and memorable weddings to come. The historic event occurred in Milwaukee, Wisconsin, where Miss Hattie Baldwin and Mr. W. McGrath exchanged vows while gliding gracefully on roller skates.

Hattie Baldwin and W. McGrath embarked on a journey that would become etched in the annals of roller skating history. With family and friends gathered to witness their union, the couple embraced the unconventional nature of their wedding, opting for a celebration that reflected their shared passion for roller skating.

As the strains of music filled the air and the couple took to the rink, they demonstrated grace and agility as they skated hand in hand, symbolizing the harmony and unity of their love. With each glide and twirl, they affirmed their commitment to one another, weaving together the threads of their lives in a joyous celebration of matrimony.

The significance of this momentous occasion was further underscored by its recognition by the National Museum of Roller Skating in Lincoln, Nebraska. By commemorating the first recorded marriage on roller skates, the museum pays homage to the enduring legacy of roller skating as a beloved pastime and cultural phenomenon.

The marriage of Hattie Baldwin and W. McGrath on roller skates serves as a reminder that love knows no bounds and that weddings can be as unique and individual as the couples themselves. Their story continues to inspire couples to embrace creativity, spontaneity, and adventure as they embark on the journey of marriage together.

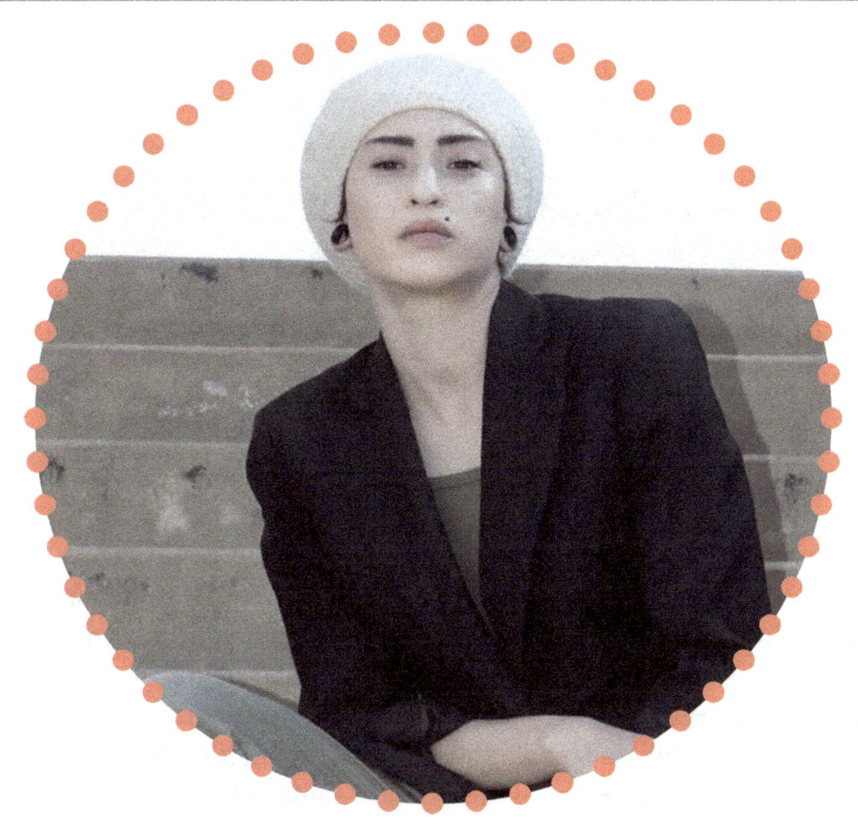

Lorraine Delarosa

aka Cherry Bomb Lips

Instagram: @rollergirl_cherrybombskates

"Miraculous Comeback"

I am a professional roller skater who is fighting paralysis. I do not have any feeling in my legs. In 2015, I survived colon cancer. I had an appointment at UCLA Children's Hospital to ring the bell that I was cancer free, but I never made it to the appointment in Los Angeles.

That morning, my family and I had just entered onto the 58 Highway in Bakersfield, California. I saw the car behind us hitting every car in its way. Unbeknownst to us, the man in the car had just caught his wife cheating on him at the country club golf course with his best friend, who was also a doctor. It turned out the man who hit the car we were riding in was one of my local cancer doctors whom I had seen the year before.

We were in the last car he hit as he drove down the freeway at a speed of 100 miles per hour. He hit our vehicle and then backed up and hit us again. This was when the car we were in exploded and the front of the doctor's car exploded while on the top of our hood. Police and an ambulance were on the scene. The impact of the accident left me paralyzed on the side of the road. Three minutes went by before I started breathing again. The policeman thought I was dead. I also lost hearing in my right ear and vision in my right eye. Things have never been the same since.

I have learned to deal with what I have left and learned to love my scars. In the last five years, I have been going through glass removal from parts of my body. At first, I didn't want anyone to see my skin

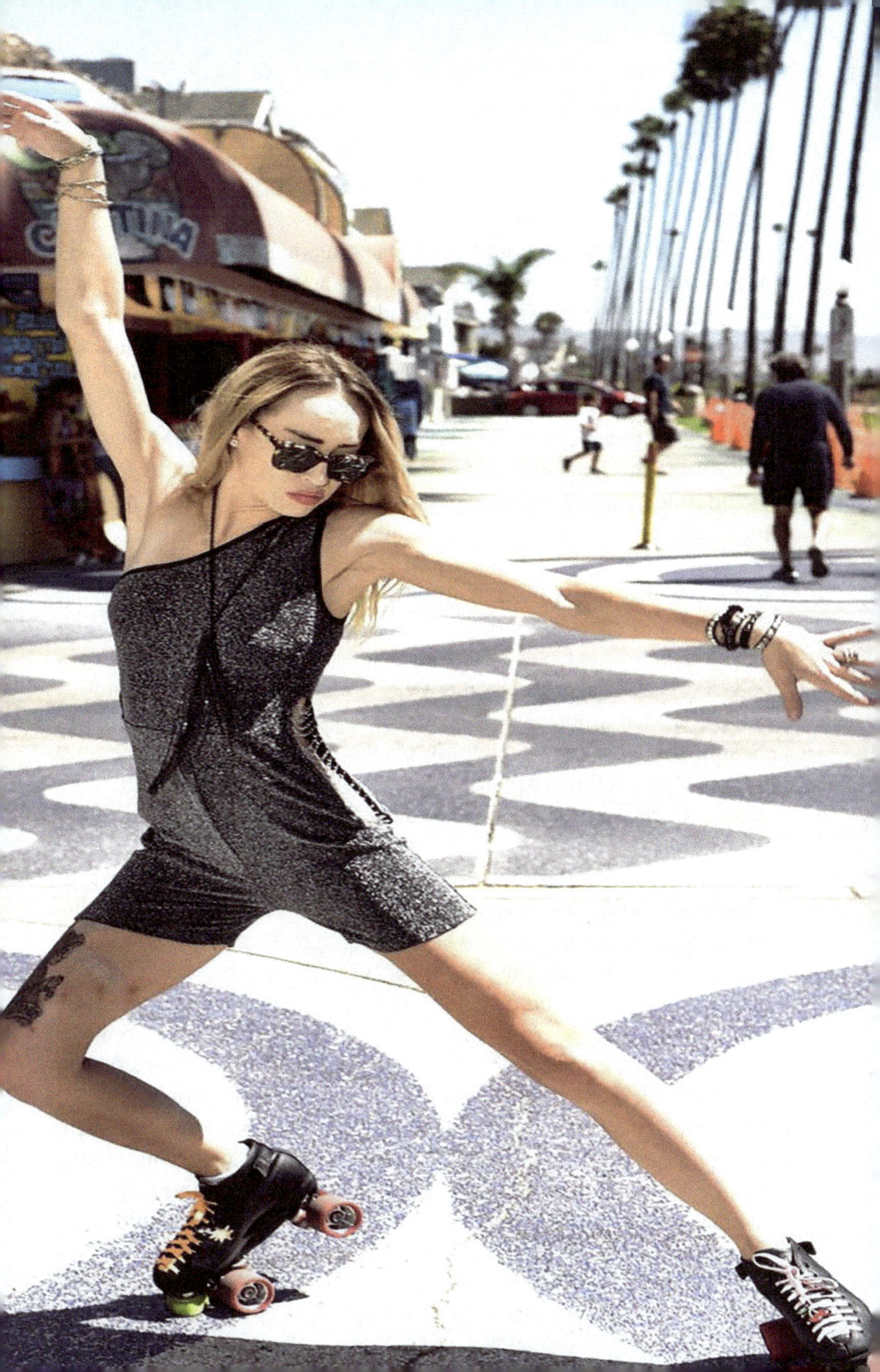

and how ugly and deep my scars and burns were. After all the therapy I went through, I learned to walk again, run again, and, most of all my, favorite thing in the world, roller skate again.

The doctors said I would never walk again, so roller skating was out of the question. I would ask and ask my primary doctor if he thought I would ever skate again and he said, "Look, kid, I am not going to tell you again. You will be lucky if you ever walk again. Be grateful you are even alive and live the rest of what you've got left in peace, alright?" I was told I would not live to see age eighteen.

After that conversation, I was devastated. I would go down to the rink, sit in my wheelchair, and just watch people skate. I had a dream I would roller skate again. I never gave up. After three years of therapy, I learned to walk. Then run. Then roller skate.

Roller skating saved me from depression and it sure made me feel somewhat like myself again. Roller skating would help me stop thinking, and even forgetting, about everything I had been through and everything that was taken from me. Roller skating has always been my safe place, my home away from home. After learning to walk, I was in a hurry to get back on my roller skates. I wanted to do something or make a name for myself again, but this time coming back with something different, a style of skating I had never done before. Back then, before the accident, I was a roller derby girl on a world-ranked team.

When I was in my wheelchair, people would ask, "If you ever come back, what are you going to do?" I was asking myself this same question in 2021. How was I going to make my comeback into roller skating after having fought cancer and being in such a bad car accident? I was hard on myself at first, telling myself that my dreams would never happen. I woke up one day with a message from OC Fashion Week, asking if I would perform on my roller skates during fashion week in swimwear for a famous designer. At the time I got the direct message, I had an air boot on my right foot. I had a broken right foot, and this was two weeks from wanting to skate at a fashion show. This was the only time I felt like not having feelings in my legs was like a superpower. I never felt any pain in my foot, but it would swell up and turn all kinds of colors.

I trained for this event on a broken foot; I was excited about the opportunity and would tell myself that I would not let my health stop me from doing this. I was very determined to skate in the fashion show no matter what it took. On the day of the fashion show, I taped up my foot with medical tape and put it in my roller skate boot. I tied the roller skate very tight and sat and waited for my music to come on. I performed for about five mins on a broken foot. Right after my performance, I skated to the back and hurried to take off my roller skates. Everyone was worrying about what I was doing. No one knew I was skating on a broken foot until after the show. It was an amazing moment for me, so it was something I would not pass up. Roller skating at the fashion show was an amazing opportunity. I made a lot of amazing friends and connections; it was an achievement and confirmation that, yes, I can do this.

After fashion week, I received a call to model for Scotty Moson on my roller skates. Making a comeback on roller skates in a fashion show helped open doors for me in the skating and modeling worlds. I finally felt like a win after everything I had gone through. Things were happening for me and I was determined to make a difference in and for the roller skating community.

During this time, I kept telling myself there is a reason for everything and there is a reason this is happening to me. I worked so hard to get back on my skates. I wanted to show the world that no matter what happened to me, I was still here, standing strong, with all my scars and burns. Deaf and blind, I was here. I was going to make my mark! I wanted to show the world that roller skating really could change someone's life positively. Roller skating is a lifestyle like no other. No matter your nationality, shape, or size, roller skating is for everyone. I have found a way of connecting with people from all over the world by roller skating on social media. I have found a few other ladies that also deal with some health problems. We found a way to make roller skating a workout for us and mental therapy. We get together about once or twice a month and roller skate and teach each other new things.

I love passing on my old tricks to my new friends. This allows me to share what I learned from my godmother, Natalie Dunn. She was a world-champion roller skater. She always told me to teach out of the goodness of my heart. Never take, just give, and always be humble. I am always willing to teach anyone who wants to learn roller skating and has a passion for it. When I came back to roller skating, I never thought I would come back to coaching and teaching again, but it is a love that's like a magnet. I love teaching and love to watch people learn to skate. Nothing makes me happier than to watch my students grow. Teaching roller skating is a way for me to connect with people from all over the world. Roller skating is my connection to the world in a very deep way.

I have, and still do, receive positive messages from people all over the world from people telling me I am an inspiration to them. The messages would say stuff like I caused them to do something positive and made them want to skate more often. I also got a lot of messages saying that my story changed their way of thinking and made them more grateful for life. My journey, persistence, and determination have affected a lot of roller skaters and people around the world. It has allowed many individuals to gain perspective and believe that if I can overcome the hardships I have faced, they, too, can make it through whatever they are experiencing and eventually reach a better place.

Roller skating gave me an outlet. It gave me a dream, and hope for better days. Roller skating changed my life for the better and made me who I am today. Roller skating is my life. I dream about roller skating every night and when I wake up and put my roller skates on, I am living my dreams.

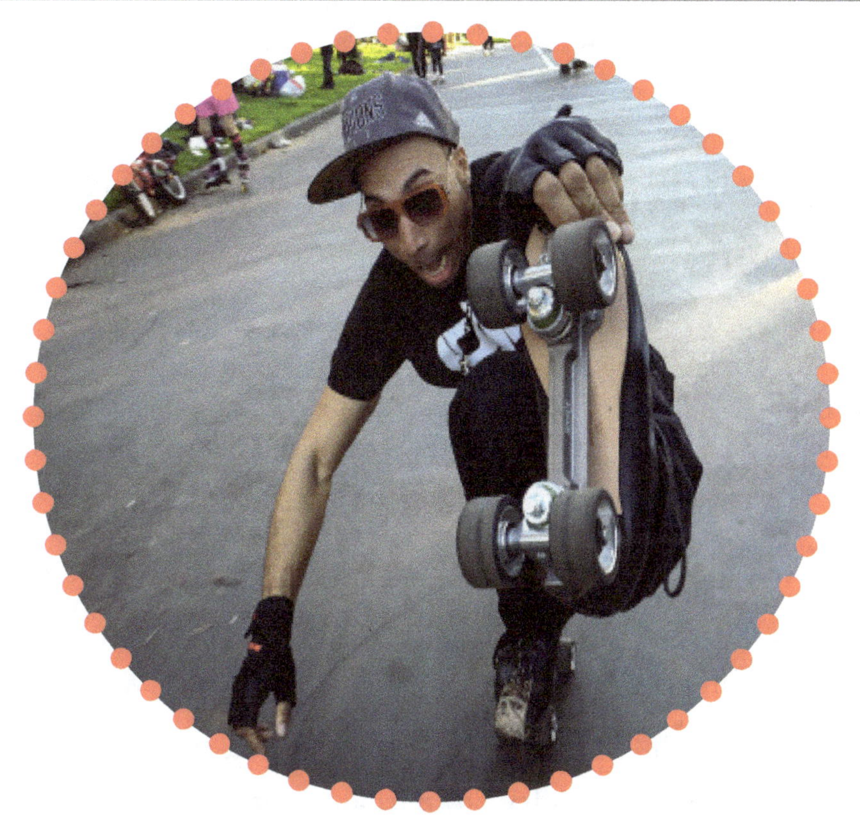

Roberto Lopez

aka Beto "Mooncricket" Lopez

Facebook: @Beto Lopez | Instagram: @mooncricketfilms

"The Art of Freestyle"

I fondly recall my first pair of skates at the age of 5—metal ones that sparked joy as I glided along the sidewalk. By age 6, I was lacing up for the first time, captivated by the fusion of music and movement that left me yearning for more. Roller skating and music became inseparable in my mind; skating without music was unimaginable. Even during my sponsorship by Roces in my early 20s, I made sure to bring my trusty old-school boombox to skate parks, ensuring that music was always part of the experience.

During my high school years, I had a massive 45-foot-long, 10-foot-high half pipe in my backyard, where music was a constant companion. Whether sliding down handrails or grinding on ramps, I infused my skating with elements of dance, busting b-boy poses and executing popping and body waves with each movement. Every time I lace up my skates, I'm transported back to that same exhilarating feeling of childhood wonder and excitement.

I've been skating since 1979 and became a serious skater in 1981; all I wanted to do was skate at the roller rinks. I made sure all my birthday parties and summer breaks were at the rink, including my sister; we always had fun. In 1983, 84, and 85, I was always popping and breaking at school and at home with friends, and in the roller rink, they would say "rex skaters only" during certain songs like Herbie Hancock's "Rocket" or Newcleus' "Jam on it." I would be popping on roller skates. Kids laughed at me, and to this very day, I still never cared about what people think.

It wasn't until the rise of social media that I finally felt recognized and respected by the roller skating community for my unique style.

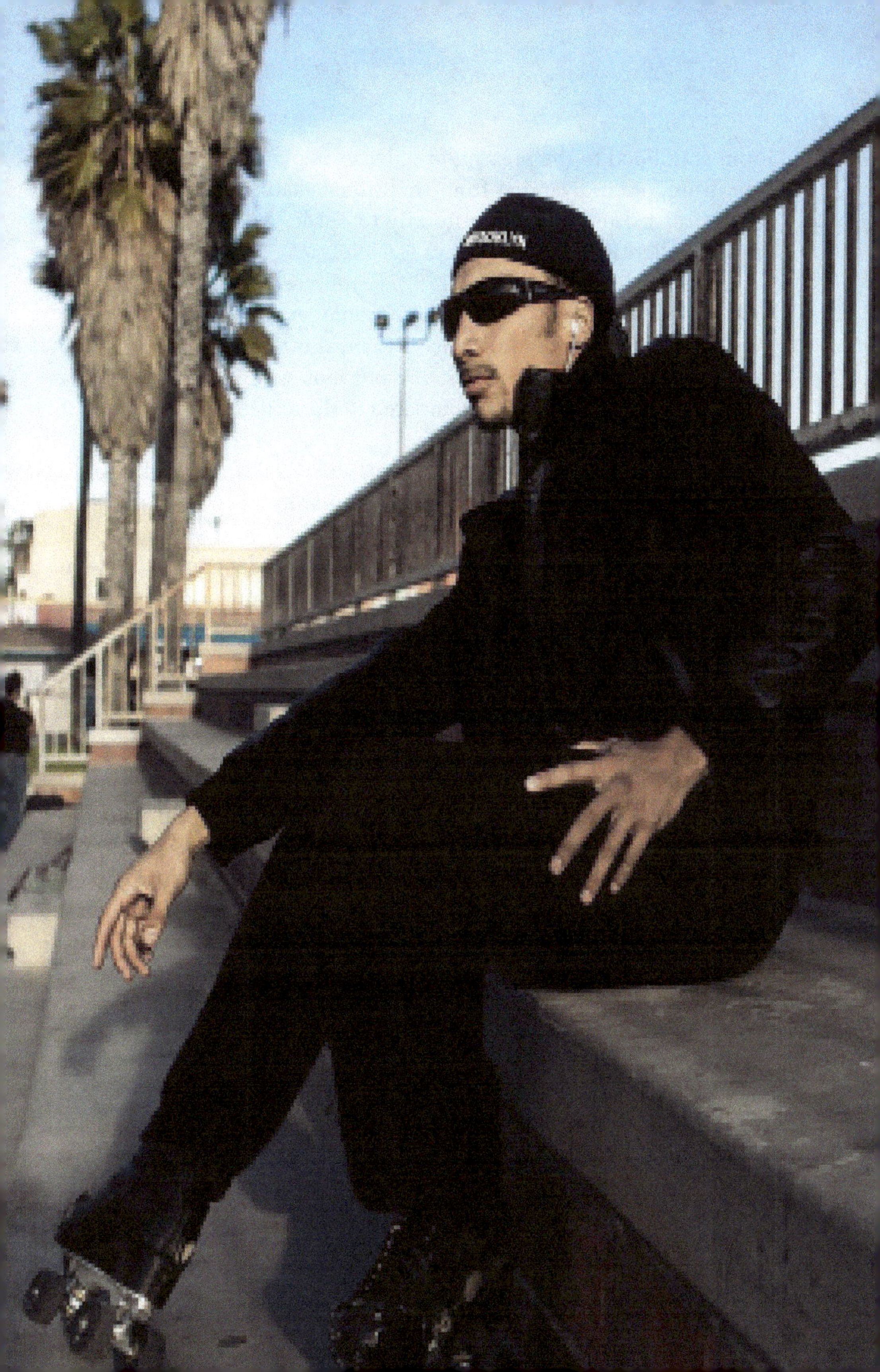

From childhood to the present, I've always marched to the beat of my own drum, often diverging from traditional skating norms. Financial constraints led me to adapt primarily to outdoor skating, as frequent visits to roller rinks weren't always feasible.

In the early 1990s, around 1992, I embraced inline skating, both indoors and outdoors. I frequented iconic spots like Golden Gate Park in San Francisco and Venice Beach, shuttling between the two despite the higher gas expenses. The outdoor skating scene offered a different energy and freedom compared to the structured environment of indoor rinks.

Indoor skating came with its own set of rules and restrictions, with rink owners occasionally voicing complaints when I incorporated breakdance moves into my routines, whether on traditional quad skates or inline skates. Despite the challenges, dancing at Golden Gate Park and Venice Beach to diverse music genres allowed me to express myself freely on wheels.

The outdoor skate community quickly embraced me, becoming my skate family. To this day, I still feel a deep connection to them, as if we've grown up together on wheels.

In 1995, I was sponsored by Roces aggressive inline skates, marking a significant milestone in my skating journey. I embarked on a traveling adventure, cruising around various local cities in my 1978 Cutlass, towing a trailer loaded with skate ramps and rails that I had meticulously crafted for my stunt performances.

Throughout the 90s, I immersed myself in skate dance contests and stunt competitions, showcasing my skills and passion for the sport. One of the standout events was the 1996 N.I.S.S. in San Francisco, sponsored by Roces, where I demonstrated my prowess.

A pinnacle moment came in 1999 when I clinched first place in the Red Bull roller dance contest in San Diego, earning a prize of $500. This victory propelled me to the world finals held on the iconic Venice Beach, where elite skaters, Chris and Dee Upshaw and others from around the globe competed on a slippery stage. Despite initial stage fright, I found my rhythm and delivered a memorable performance.

Subsequently, I continued to dazzle audiences through contest appearances, stage performances, and concerts, sharing the spotlight with renowned artists like Shannon Green and Newcleus. Having honed my skills in dancing and rapping on stage since elementary and high school, skating brought forth a unique energy and passion that resonated deeply with me.

Today, my skating style reflects elements of performance art, earning recognition from spectators who appreciate the fusion of athleticism and creativity in my skating.

Skating for me is more than just a hobby—it's a passion that allows me to connect with others, spread joy, and inspire those around me. One of my most cherished roles is performing for Velocity Circus in San Francisco, where I've had the privilege of entertaining audiences at major corporate events such as the Oracle conference and holiday parties for prominent tech companies. However, due to the pandemic, many of these opportunities have been put on hold.

My skate style, which I like to call "The Art of Freestyle," is deeply rooted in musicality and expression. I thrive on dancing to various genres of music, adapting my movements to match the rhythm and mood. While I steer clear of overly silly tunes, I embrace the opportunity to synchronize my entire body with the music, translating its energy into fluid transitions, spins, and dynamic poses reminiscent of a b-boy ready to break into every move.

Smoothness is key in my skating style, as I strive to seamlessly blend different elements into a captivating performance. Whether it's conveying a specific emotion or showcasing my skills as a performer, I aim to create visually compelling moments that resonate with viewers. Making people smile is my ultimate goal, and there are times when I become so immersed in the music that I lose myself in the moment.

However, like any passionate skater, I have my pet peeves. One of them is being interrupted while I'm in the zone, especially when I'm about to execute a complex spin or floor move. While I enjoy teaching and sharing my knowledge with others, there are moments when I simply want to fully immerse myself in the music and movement without distractions.

I've innovated my teaching approach by integrating principles of body language and balance that I learned from the late Shabba Doo of the Lockers, particularly in the art of "Locking." While I frequently incorporate Locking into my skate performances, I also use it as a foundational technique in my skate dance classes to illustrate its versatility across various music genres, including slow funk and hip-hop. By sharing these techniques, I empower skaters to develop their own unique style and identity, enabling them to stand out on platforms like Instagram and TikTok.

Inspired by the teachings of Richard Humphrey, who encouraged me to infuse my personal style into his techniques, I've embraced a fusion approach to skating. While some may categorize me solely as a b-boy due to my breaking and popping skills on skates, my repertoire extends far beyond that. I draw inspiration from an eclectic mix of influences, including James Brown, Otis Redding, salsa, jazz, tap, and more, resulting in a fusion of dance styles on roller skates.

I often refer to myself as a "skate fusion" artist, as my performances encompass elements from a diverse range of dance styles. While I'm adept at learning choreography, I'm typically driven to improvise and express myself when my favorite songs play. Although I enjoy teaching choreography, my passion lies in guiding students to develop their musicality and interpretive skills, ultimately fostering their ability to create their own unique skating style. Instead of relying solely on counts, I encourage students to connect with the rhythm and sounds of the music, allowing them to express themselves authentically on the rink.

My most memorable moments would be the four years in a row going to Skate Love Barcelona and teaching a class there. Meeting international skaters from around the world and feeling like a world skate family was a blessing. Living in China for 6 months in 2016-2017, skating the streets everywhere to film for the job I was doing and filming myself skating in the most beautiful locations in many cities of China.

I'd like to note my preferred skate setup, which consists of Riedell 336 boots paired with Reactor plates, Roller Bone 101 wheels, and bearings. I've specifically selected wheels with a 101 hardness and a diameter of 57mm, ideal for both indoor and outdoor skating, particularly for dancing. However, when skating around the local lake in Oakland or embarking on long rides along trails and sidewalks, I opt for softer outdoor wheels to enhance maneuverability and comfort.

Many individuals often inquire about which wheels they should choose for their skates. In response, I emphasize that the selection largely depends on their intended skating activities. For instance, if they plan to engage in various activities like myself, including both indoor and outdoor skating, I recommend wheels that offer versatility and adaptability across different surfaces and environments.

I'm frequently asked about my favorite song to skate to, and my response is that I have many favorites, each suited to different styles and categories of music. When it comes to a slow jam, I have a particular favorite that transports me to another realm, where I close my eyes and feel the music deep within. If it's funk, the right song will evoke images of dancers from Soul Train, and I'll break into a locking frenzy. Classic hip-hop tunes from artists like Gang Starr or Big Daddy Kane inspire me to skate and dance with a 90s flair, incorporating ground moves reminiscent of b-boy breaking. As for new hip-hop, I don't always keep track of song names or artists; instead, I tune into the basic beats and let the music guide my movements. There are a few tracks, though, that stick in my mind, often heard at the rinks I frequent, prompting me to explore new moves. I particularly enjoy songs with breaks that signal the perfect moment for a fast or extended spin, followed by a dramatic freeze. One such favorite is Kool and the Gang's "Summer Madness," with its iconic keyboard pitch ascending higher and higher, urging me to spin faster and faster. Anything with this dynamic quality in music captivates me on skates.

When asked why I skate with such passion and dedication, I often find myself reflecting on the profound impact skating has had on my life. In many ways, skating has been my salvation, offering solace and healing during some of my darkest moments. Like many, my upbringing was fraught with challenges and trauma, but through it all, skating emerged as my most potent form of therapy and lifeline. The absence of skating, whether due to broken skates or injury, leaves me feeling adrift and vulnerable. While I have plenty to occupy my mind, the inability to skate for even a short period can plunge me into a state of sadness. Skating serves as a powerful escape from reality, a realm where negativity and troubles dissipate in the exhilarating embrace of movement and music. When I'm on my skates, particularly to the rhythm of uplifting music, I am enveloped in a profound sense of joy and gratitude for life. However, there are moments on the rink floor when a love song triggers memories of someone dear to me, evoking a bittersweet ache. Yet, rather than suppress these emotions, I choose to embrace them, allowing the music to guide my movements as I express the depth of my feelings through skating. Sometimes, this immersion in emotion is so intense that spectators are moved to tears, unaware that I, too, am navigating a whirlwind of sentiments beneath the surface. In those fleeting moments, I transcend the confines of the rink, channeling the passion and intensity of an Olympic athlete, albeit in my own humble way.

Those familiar with me are aware of a unique ability I possess—a hidden superpower, if you will. I have the remarkable gift of remembering my lucid dreams with astonishing clarity. Not only can I recall these dreams with precision, but I have the ability to traverse multiple dreamscapes and recall dreams dating back to when I was four years old. If prompted, I can delve into the vast repository of my dream experiences and recount them in vivid detail. However, given the sheer depth of these dreams, such narratives tend to be short and concise, as they encompass a lifetime's worth of powerful and intricately woven dreams. As for my legacy, I aspire to be remembered as more than just a passionate skater, but as someone deeply committed to uplifting and uniting my community. Organizing events has been a labor of love for me since the early 90s, and witnessing people come together, gliding to music, fills me with immense joy. I cherish the opportunity to foster connections and create memorable experiences. Beyond skating, my other passion lies in filmmaking. Through documentaries, videos, and photography, I strive to capture the essence of roller skating culture. My current roller skate documentary, Sk8 Fever, is not just a personal project, but a historical record that I hope will be preserved for generations to come. It is a tribute to the individuals whose stories I have had the privilege to document, spanning across the globe. Their narratives deserve to be immortalized, much like the captivating book series authored by Amirah Palmer that you are currently enjoying.

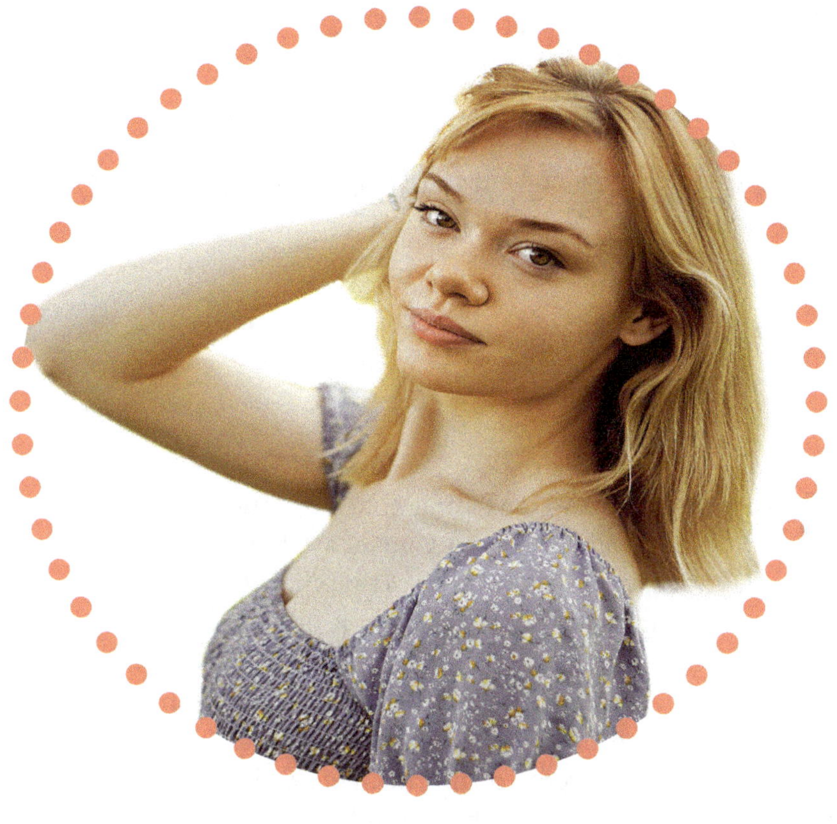

Haleigh Gross

Facebook: @Haleigh Gross | Instagram: @haleighgross

"Skating Was My First Love"

Have you ever had something that you know you were born to do? Something so dear to your heart that no matter how hard you tried, you'd never be able to explain what it means to you? That's what skating is for me. It quite literally is one of the first things I ever learned how to do, alongside walking, talking, and a bunch of other firsts that would come later in life. Unlike most parents who just had their firstborn, my mom and dad didn't go straight home afterward. Instead, my parents went to the rink where they had grown up and introduced me to the place that would become my home. Even at a young age, it brought such a powerful sense of love and belonging. It was addicting. Even so young, I knew I would have a place to go if I were to have nothing. I formed some of the greatest relationships inside my rink.

I met friends, best friends, even people who would become aunts and uncles to me. I was surrounded by love when I stepped in, which is why I spent my entire childhood in a skating rink, weaving in and out of adults and showing off to any kid my age. As with most little kids, I absolutely loved showing off to people. Skating may have given me a bit of a superiority complex, but I can admit that for my age, I was better than most kids. Every little kid has something they show off at recess, whether it's soccer, football, or even the coolest gymnastics tricks. While I obviously couldn't skate at recess, I could flaunt my skills at the monthly skating parties. When I tell you these were the highlights

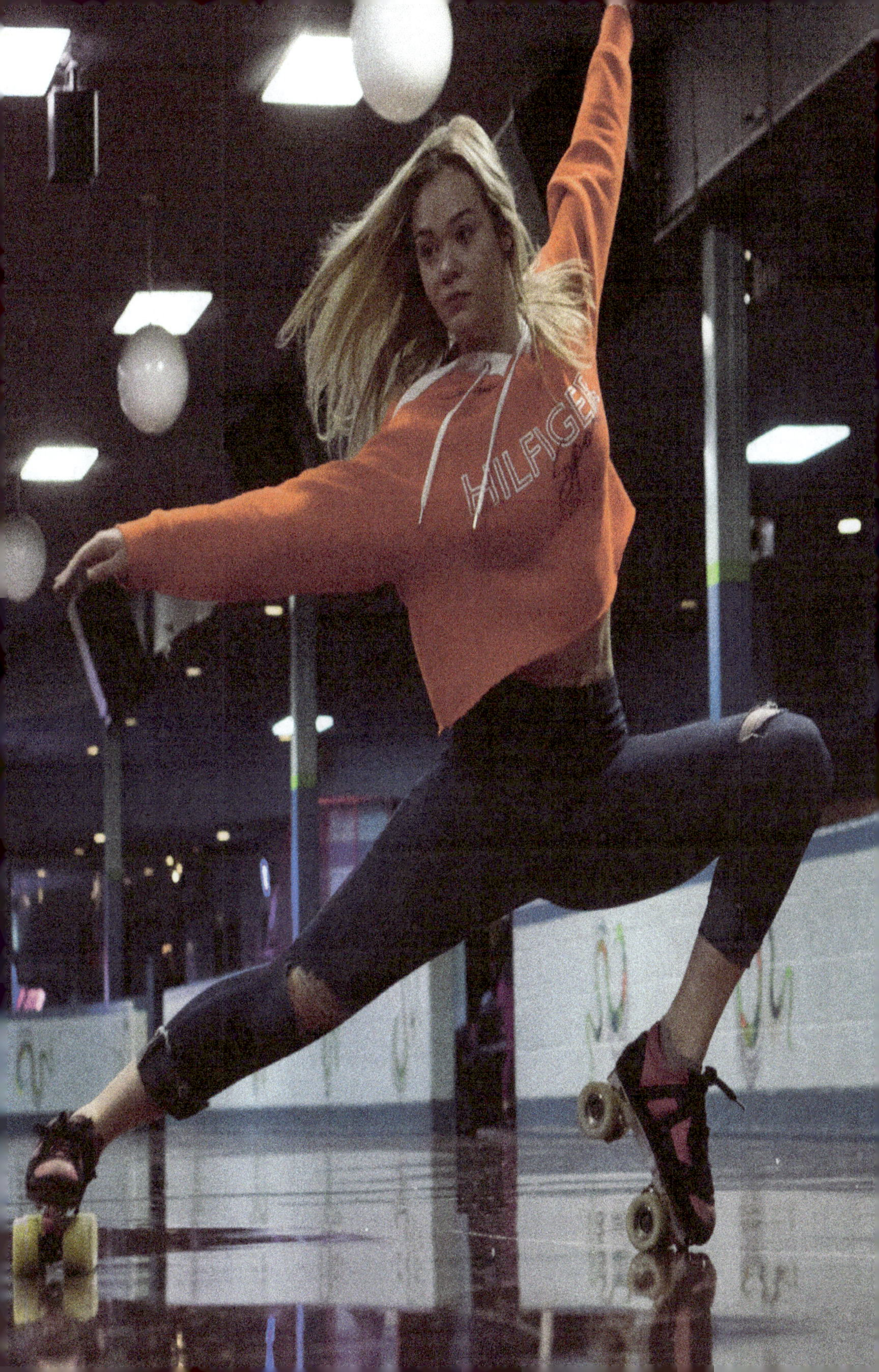
HILFIGER

of my elementary and middle school years; I regularly lost sleep over being so excited. I actually made most of my friends at these parties and I cherish the memories I made at them.

This may seem miniscule, but it has a point. Skating is attached to so many memories and milestones, like birthday parties and even my first job. That's right, those firsts I mentioned earlier that would come later in life? Not only was skating my first love, one of those firsts is my job as well. I actually turned in my application as a joke. I was only fourteen and my parents, who worked at my rink, gave me an application but I didn't think anything would happen. Yet sure enough, five years later I'm still there. These past five years at my job have been amazing, from having the pleasure of watching little kids grow up to seeing adults tear up the skate floor during sessions with old friends. Some of my favorite times at my job involve when adults tell me how much they enjoyed skating when they were young or how they ended up meeting their best friend or future spouse at a skating rink. This is where I've seen how skating and its culture have affected others. I've been to so many birthday and graduation parties for people of all ages. I've seen marriage proposals, even had the chance to go to a vow renewal at my rink! The term "skate family" is like no other word in the English language, or any language really. I have never seen a community so supportive and uplifting, so welcoming and loving.

It's an honor to be a part of it. It's a tight-knit community that is parallel to none. When the Dayton tornadoes struck, I knew of skate friends that got together and spent the day cleaning up debris. I've also known people that held fundraisers to support other skaters. Most heartwarming of all is when skaters come together for a memorial skate, reminiscing and treasuring our loved skate family member and keeping their memory alive. I could go on and on, but I believe I've made my point. A skate family isn't a "second family," it's just a family where all are welcome and we are connected with one love. I am so grateful to be a part of something as incredible as this and I know for sure I will raise my future kids to be a part of it as well. The adults I have met through my years of skating have been very influential in my life. They've given me wisdom and advice I will remember for the rest of my life. Some wisdom I clearly remember being told was, "The world was born to skate. Whether people push it away or forget about it, skating will be there for those who need it. Skate culture will always be present."

Despite being so young when told this, it has stuck with me for over ten years. I always wondered what this person meant. As a little girl, I had absolutely no idea what skate culture comprised. In fact, I didn't even know it existed. I knew I could skate, that I liked skating, and that it was popular in the seventies and eighties, but really that was about it. What did they mean? The answer would come when I was fifteen. Up to that point I had only worn inline skates. I had been involved in speed skating when I was younger but quit, yet I never made the transition to quads until 2017. I had some friends push me toward them and my skate life was changed forever. I discovered a new side of skating I never knew existed. First discovered was jam skating. I was obsessed with the high energy, the intense battles, hyping up the crowd and getting them involved, and an impressive set of tricks I didn't even know were possible on skates. I mean come on, a backflip? That is literally the most insane thing ever. Anyway, jam skating was just the door to the realm of skate styles. I worked tirelessly to be good at it. My fifteen years of dance really helped me out and a year after I started, I was grateful to be offered a sponsorship. Now that looks good on college resumes! If you're not familiar with jam skating, throughout the year, different competitions take place across the country, and skaters "battle" one another, usually for cash prizes. There are many different categories like 1v1s or 3v3s, even musicality, and others on top of that. My first (and only) competition would be the Jingle Jam in 2019, taking place at my home rink. During this time, I got to take classes from skating legends and even watch them compete. I took the chance to get out of my comfort zone and compete, and won my battle! Even cooler was the fact that not one but two videos of mine went viral on TikTok! After that weekend, I had so many people tell me I make them want to skate again, which might be the compliment that hits me the most. That weekend really kick-started my determination to share skating with the world. If there's anything I want to achieve in life, it's getting people to discover love in skating. Sadly, that determination didn't last long as the world shut down less than three months later. The one thing that really hit me hard during COVID was not being able to skate.

Skating was my outlet. Sure, I skated outside, but it was nowhere near the feeling of being inside a rink. Being able to get lost in the music and have my friends around me was something I took for granted. Not to mention skating on a smooth surface. Those pebbles can really get you. My determination to get better was shot, and I thought I had lost my love for skating. Eventually, the world opened back up, and yet I could not get myself to the rink. As cliche as this may sound, I truly started questioning who I was. I invested my whole life in skating just to stop like that? I knew I had it in me. I just didn't know how to get it back. The jam skating community seemed barren at the time, and this would eventually lead me to rhythm skating.

Rhythm skating was so special to me with the way everything flowed and was connected. Even more notable was that I saw it all over Instagram. Once again, I was obsessed and motivated and finally ready to get my skates back on. I even bought some high-tops, a pair of Riedell Angels, that were so different from my previous skate I didn't know if I could pull them off, but my Angels have become my best friend. After discovering rhythm skating came JB skating, and much more. As I learn more about the different skate styles, there is always an underlying factor that makes me realize why I adore skating. There really is no wrong way to skate. If there's one thing I love, it's that it's so versatile that it's something you can make your own. There are no rules, no limits, no boundaries that can stop you. Creativity is endless and, as someone who needs a creative outlet, skating is my perfect match.

Inspiration is at every corner (or should I say rink) and you'll always have support, whether in person or virtually. There is no sense of competition in skating, just bettering yourself, others, and the community as a whole. From my experience in many different sports and art, that aspect is extremely unique. What is also unique is that age doesn't stop someone from skating. From toddlers to the elderly and everyone in between, they're able to get on eight wheels and roll. You cannot tell me your heart doesn't melt when you see an elderly couple skate together. Adults have asked me if it's too late for them to start and my answer is always *no*. Anyone and everyone can discover the joy of skating. I could go on and on about my love for it, but then this may get too long. To wrap this up, whether you use it for exercise, a family activity, a way to make new friends, or anything else, skating is there for everyone to enjoy in any way they see fit. It provides a nurturing environment for all those involved. If I could leave one last note for anyone that reads this, it's to share your passion with the world. Inspire others to skate and spread the love that comes with it. One of my hopes in life is to see skating grow back to the popularity it had years ago and I believe it's on that path currently. With the help of the skating community, I've pushed through intense fears of judgment to start sharing my own passion for skating, and I believe we all as a family need to share that love and passion we adore so much to inspire and prove to everyone that the world truly was born to skate.

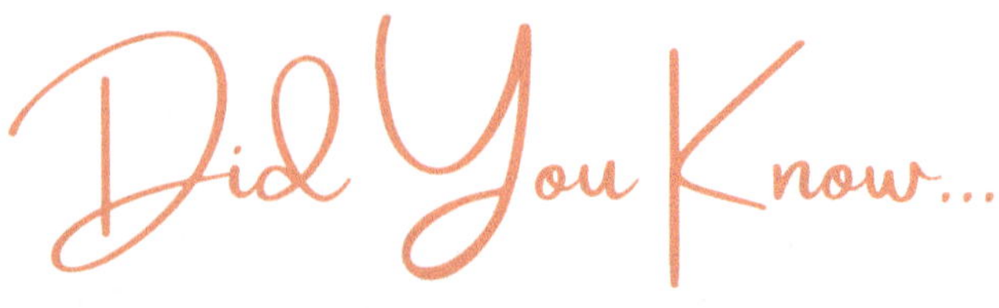

National Roller Skating Museum

Established in 1980, the National Museum of Roller Skating provides the public with an experience to reflect on and understand the sport of roller skating and its history. With exhibits containing artifacts dating back to the early 19th century, the museum presents roller skating throughout the years.

The museum's grand opening to the public was on April 13th, 1982, and houses the largest collection of roller skating items in the world and the National Roller Skating Archives, which contains publications and information on the people, objects, and events connected to roller skating's history.

Source: Skating museum: National museum of rollerskating: United states. National Museum of Roller Skating. (1982, April 13). https://www.rollerskatingmuseum.org/

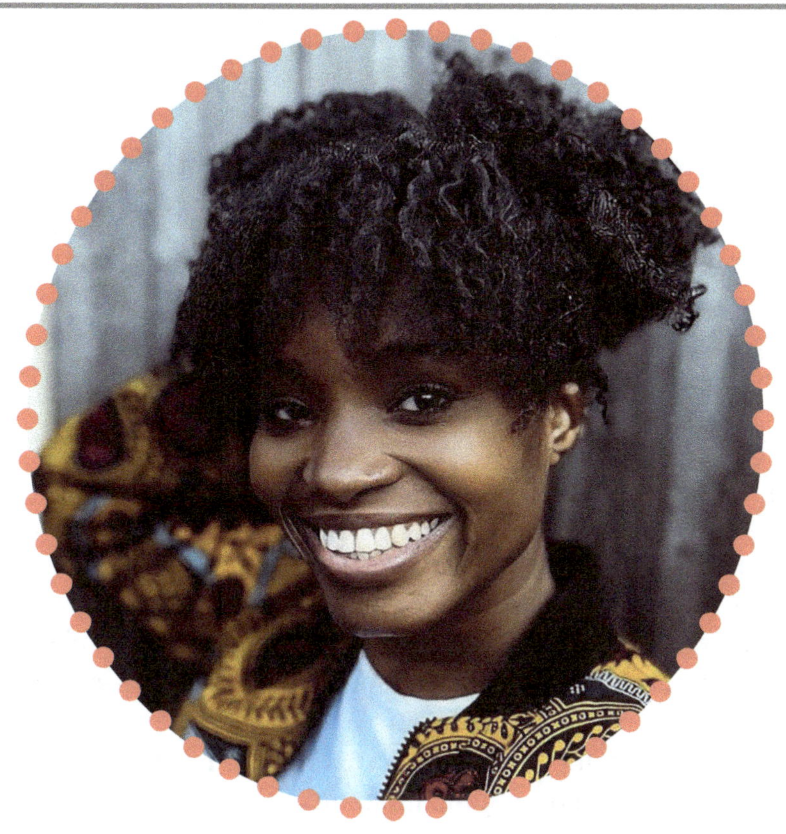

Tendai Chagweda

aka Petit DJ

Facebook: Tendai Chagweda | Instagram: @PetiteDJ

"I Did Everything On My Skates"

My name is Tendai. My name means "Thankful to God" and I'm of Zimbabwean origin/roots. I was born and raised in South London, UK, in a very small knit family. I was nicknamed Titch and then Petite in my neighborhood and that name later became my MC then DJ name. On the skate scene, some call me Aunty—an endearing term to call elders (female, of course).

Unlike most of the awesome stories I've read in this book series, my skate journey began during the infamous COVID pandemic. Ishariah Johnson aka Storm Skater, one of the first professional skaters I met here in London, called us the "Corona Rollers," since we sprung into skating when the "Coronavirus" happened, and I still love that term to this day. Many don't, but, hey. Prior to the pandemic, no one in my family skated, so my passion for skating was self-created. I begged for a pair of skates for my ninth or tenth birthday and was over the moon when I got the Fisher-Price expandable ones, and then my gray and blue-striped trainer boot skates. But I grew out of them quickly, and I remember forcing myself into them despite the pinch. I'm surprised I didn't get blisters because I forced them on so I could get the last few skates out of them. I don't even have a picture of them, that's how briefly I had them, but I know I loved doing lemons in them. I have no idea who taught me, but I remember how great it felt doing them, going forward and backward. This move would aid me in my later years.

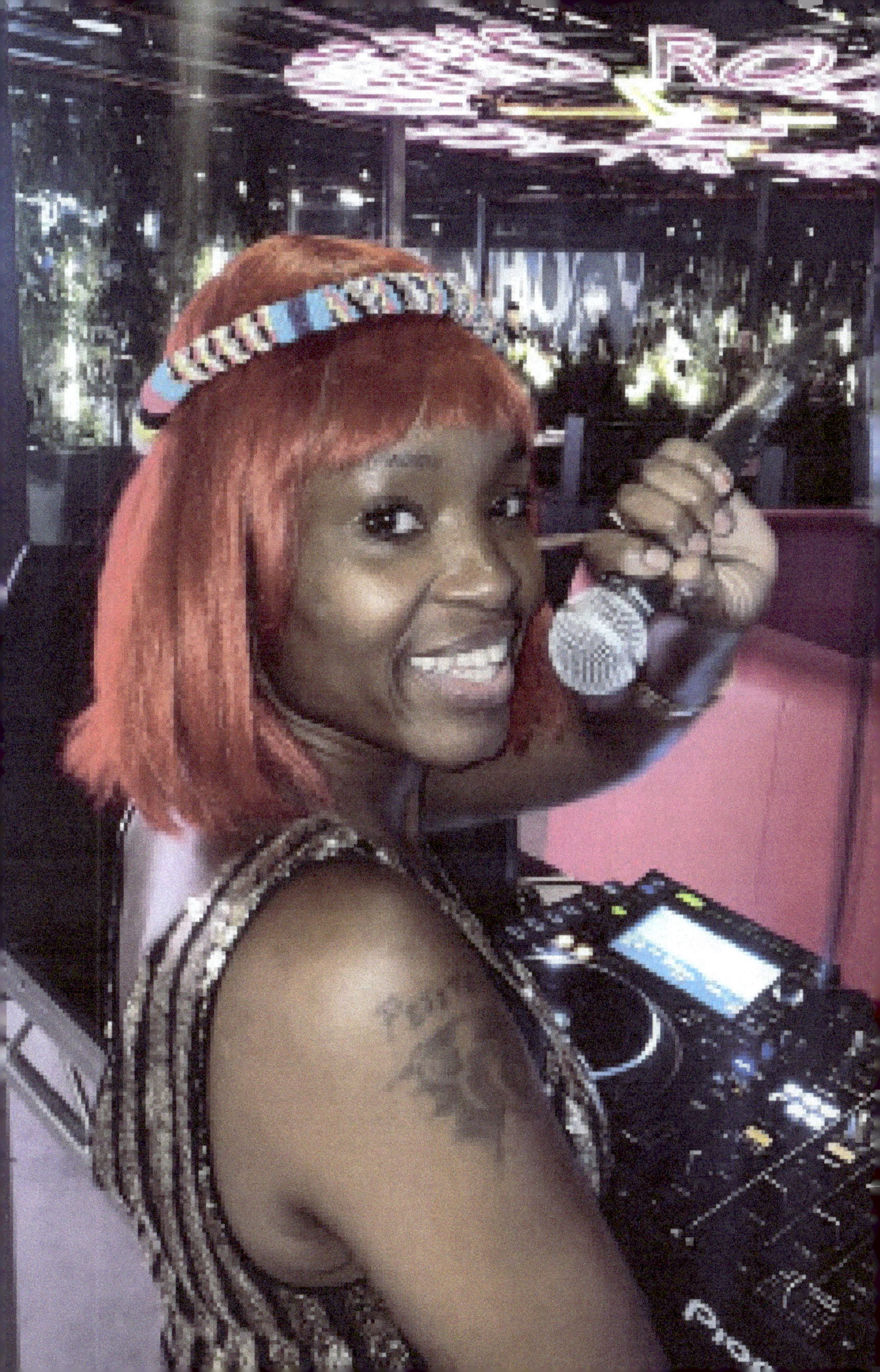

No one around me skated or had skates. There was no rink that I knew of, so my childhood skate period was super brief. I went to someone's birthday party at Roller Express in Vauxhall, South London, later in my teens, but enjoyed the raving scene far too much to appreciate how good skating was, plus the music was not doing it for me. I was addicted to the mic back then and loved sneaking on stage with DJs, so the skating went over my head that day.

Music has always been a big thing for me. I played trombone, baritone, and clarinet from eight years old and I somehow had a gift for brass 'instruments'. I wouldn't practice a lot, but when I played, it was effortless, and I'd get called to play at school solos for assemblies and special events. This was when I first realized that I struggled with practicing/doing things for long periods of time, even if I loved doing it/something. My brain physically switches off and I get worse and worse the more I try. So doing things I pick up effortlessly is really important to me. If I have to put in too much effort, my brain and body give up. I like to grasp things instantly. Math, reading, music, board games, and learning Spanish, I was able to do effortlessly and without much practice. Everything else is pretty much a struggle and a few people pointed out I may have ADHD. I brushed it off as I'd got great GCSEs without having to study. I went on to study accounting qualifications in college as I wanted the easy option (for me), working with numbers! I realized it made sense to follow what I was good at, and what I loved (math).

When I got my first full-time job at American Express, without the qualifications or experience they desired, I treated myself to inline skates for me and an ex, aged nineteen (this would've been around 1999-2000) from my first ever catalogue. He'd never skated before, and I was an amateur, so we were a sorry sight together. We'd skate in Hyde Park; I had no idea this was a famous skate spot and really wish we saw skaters that could've told us some tips, but we never saw anyone but us fumbling around. The skates lasted longer than the relationship. My feet didn't grow (thank God) and I picked the skates back up ten years later.

I lived on Denmark Hill and made my way to a local park. There were hills and I had no idea that I didn't know how to stop. The first collision was into the traffic lights, that was my first warning to turn back and go home. The second collision was the stairs that I had no other option but to jump down. It was a messy fall—I nearly did the splits—there were at least eight stairs and I had to fly over all eight as I had no idea how to stop. The era of social media and filming everything on mobile phones wasn't quite there yet, fortunately, but I gave spectators a good run for their money that day. I carried on skating forward out of shame and took off the skates and walked home barefoot, eventually.

The skates stayed boxed up for another ten years. Then I skated on them every summer in my late thirties, doing Facebook lives. I'd just go to my local lake, and meet other friends. Eventually, I learned there was a stopper on the back and I was confident to cross the main road, but I was still very much an amateur. It was only when I broke my ankle in 2018 that I stopped with my annual Facebook live solo skate trips to the park. I was down, but not out.

I still can't wear high heels, but I sure as hell skate. The irony! So, I started skating again at the age of forty-two. It all started with an online vision board workshop I was running in February 2020, just before lockdown. I'm a true believer in manifesting and setting intentions, and one area of my life I knew I had to work on was my health. At forty-two years old, I hadn't seen a gym in nearly ten years and I knew this had to change. I wanted to be more active and two of my clients, Cherelle and Karlene, spoke about skating on my previous live vision board calls, so I followed suit and added some roller skates to my vision board. Cherelle got in to skating the first year we spoke about it (pre-lock down) and later Karlene advised there was a skate community in Peckham (SE London) and I knew it would be more beneficial for me skating as a collective rather than individually, so I took the steps to find this community. To no avail. A month later, the coronavirus pandemic happened, and we were instructed that we were on lockdown and not allowed to leave our homes unless we were shopping or exercising. So, I pulled out my twenty-year-old catalogue inline skates and tried to skate, but felt unstable as I'd broken my ankle two years before and one skate was missing a strap.

I purchased a pair of cheap £20 skates online to see how I'd be back on quads, and I skated to my local park. It was awful. Wrong wheels, wrong route, I wasn't used to wearing a heel on skates; the balance felt off! I was going nowhere fast and still couldn't find the skate group on or offline. One day, I was sitting down at my local lake with my skates on, on the phone with bestie, Jo Blake, and I was randomly approached by Ronaldo, one of the co-founders of the skate community I was trying to find. Wow! It's called Burgess Park skate community (BPSC) and they created a committee and organized skate meetups, WhatsApp groups and there was a real community of inline and quad skaters of all abilities. And here began my manifested skate journey. Thank you, Universe.

I upgraded to the Ventro Pro hockey boots, and despite breaking my wrist skating home from the lake that same month, I went to watch the BPSC practicing skate moves—whilst sitting on the "injury bench" with other spectators. I couldn't wait to heal and join them. Then, when I got better and stupidly decided not to wear the new (and expensive) protective gloves one day, I sprained my other hand. The pain! It was here I realized the importance of protective gear, especially for beginners and especially for street skaters. Broken bones in your older years take longer to heal. I caught "COVID" after my second hospital visit. I couldn't smell or taste anything for months.

Whilst on the sub-bench, I met two beautiful fellow Nubian skaters, CeCe and Cherry. CeCe invited me to Hyde Park, a renowned skate spot in London, to skate and we met Storm Skater jam skating with other talented jam skaters on the scene that we had no idea existed. This was my first or second day back on skates from my first injury and I tried to jam for the first time. I had no idea it wasn't easy. From there I defaulted back to park and street skating. It was too much work for me! I was still a basic skater, but hearing the music and seeing the skaters, the vibe and energy spoke to me instantly. I went back to my vision board at the end of that lock down year (2020) and knew I wanted to combine my passion for: 1. Amapiano (South African house music), 2. DJing, 3. Skating, and 4. Some form of exercise for keeping fit.

The following year 2021, I attended skate events, street skates and road trips that I never knew existed. These were hosted by Fix8 who had been running a weekly event in Wembley for nearly ten years, WavyOn8 who host the biggest attended outdoor and indoor events, WatchMyWheels who run events and skate classes, Sk8city London based in Harrow who run end-of-month skate nights, and SkateWithSis the first all-female skate events, creating safe spaces for sisters to skate and meet. I went on my first road trip to Birmingham for Sisterhood Skates with Cherry and the sisters I met in online black sisterhood groups: Chamz, Asante, Pauline, and Shalomi. I also went on my first seaside skate road trip with Ennor, Alba and Kadija—unforgettable days. By then, I had upgraded my hockey skates to Rookie Artistics, who later sponsored me with skates for a Grace Jones event at Southbank, curated by Kadija in Summer 2021.

I also teach disabled people to DJ, and I invited one of my DJs who skates to DJ alongside me—Roisin aka DJ4Blue. She smashed the booking at Southbank and she now works at Flippers, London. Cherry told me about SkateLove Barcelona but due to the global lockdown, it was being canceled that year. I tried to arrange for a group of us to go the following year, but people were dropping out and changing their mind about coming. I knew in my soul I'd be going. I'd done the research and the previous events online looked like a dream. I had to manifest it! I added SkateLove on to my vision board at the end of 2020. I nearly gave up until fellow BPSC skater "Joy" from HoopHustleFlow advised that SkateLove was looking for teachers, volunteers and DJs in April 2021! I applied immediately! I was listening to my own mixes on SoundCloud and iTunes, whilst park and street skating and it gave me a new lease on life as I'd recently retired from DJing on the non-skate circuit (combo of depression and the lack of love for Amapiano from revelers), and I was dedicated to teaching others how to DJ with my DJ school (@InspiringDJs) with my online and offline DJ classes.

As summer 2021 approached, I went to local outdoor skate locations with my DJ decks and a big speaker, which I was carrying around on buses and trains. I DJ'd for whoever was up for hearing the Amapiano music I loved. Some people hated it, but as we all know, you can't please everyone. My mission was to get seen and booked on the scene, in a scene full of many talented skaters and DJs. Becoming a skate DJ, my DJ escapades across North, East and South London got me noticed and though my traction on my social media posts were minimal, promoters and skate crews were hitting up my DMs (direct messages) to enquire and book me for their events. The exact people I wanted to work with! I noticed that a lot of the DJs that were being booked locally and internationally didn't necessarily have high followings or tractions on posts, and this gave me hope as I only had 1,000 followers on account, and 3,500 on another page (@ BlackCalendarUK) and I barely get 100 likes. It was a classic example of quality over quantity.

I wanted to DJ at the indoor and outdoor events. I supported, networked, and even jammed in the middle with zero jam skills! I attended events solo, knowing I would meet people I had met along the way on the scene. I was connecting photographers and videographers with promoters and talented skaters. One of my superpowers is connecting and networking, and identifying and using this has been instrumental in my journey.

My passion for skating had soared. I did EVERYTHING on my skates, from supermarket shopping and going to the hairdressers to securing jobs, rolling up to meetings and interviews. Quadzilla, founder of Good Foot Skates, and Von Merlin Wheels in Dallas, and the events Manager for SkateLove, loved my Amapiano mixes and DJ application and booked me to play Primetime sets at Skate Love 2021 (and then again in 2022—I hadn't even applied so I was stunned to be invited again!).

At this stage I was still a one-dimensional Amapiano and House DJ, but luckily it worked for me as no one really played the music I play. I especially loved that I was booked for the Meet n Greet sessions as the solo DJ for four hours both nights. These nights have the prominent skaters from the scene globally, coming and sharing their journey and rise to success. Oumi Janta, my fellow melanin queen that everyone tagged me as looking like—beautiful, talented skater from Berlin that went viral in lockdown, SkateFantacee creator of World Wide Rollout day (global annual movement in July), Terrell Host of TheBrickTV's "Roll Call" from Skate documentary "Roller Dreams," Florian creator of the Flaneurz skates, Kai creator of Fix8 and FlippersUK Mgmt., as well as: @michelleptybcn and Michelle Barrios @michelleptybcn and @lexmilczarek—"Roller Talents for Castings" @troubleon8wheels—

"Launching a skate shop in a pandemic" @morganweske—"Global Skate Traveler" Mo Sanders @quadzillalk- "Sponsored by Von Merlin. I met skaters I'd never heard off, and connected with skaters from Europe and USA that I was following on Instagram—Richard Humphrey, Lola the Beast, Downtown Sam, Smooth Goddess, Pooh and his wife Temptest and many others. I also met some people I had seen from the Roller Dreams documentary, which I'd watched in Theatre Peckham. The documentary touched my soul differently. I was the only one shedding tears. Seeing how skaters had taken it professionally inspired me to dig deeper, and at the 2022 SkateLove, my set times were changed super last minute. Instead of making a mountain hill of the situation I decided to introduce speed skating on my set, given the new times I had. This took away more DJing time from my reduced set, but I was keen on allowing the Londoners to skate their favorite style of skating (backward fast). There were a lot of beginners on the rink, slower skaters, skaters that couldn't speak English, skaters that wanted to cruise quietly in the afternoon sun, skaters that couldn't go backward, but I patterned it up so that it would be safe, fun and electric. I worked with one of the key London skaters, @UnseenKinochi, to make sure the floor would be safe at the time I made the announcement. I teased the skaters with the anthem speed skate song and saw a scurry of skaters stand to attention and head to the rink. I worked the mic and invited beginners to join the sea of skaters; the floor came alive with testosterone/speed and euphoric energy.

By now, you've gathered I'm a risk taker. There's more to the story, but in a nutshell, it was one of my favorite calculated risks. I'd never played anything but Amapiano on my skate sets and playing that Jungle made me come alive and since then, I've now evolved and I play JB beats, hip hop, slow jams, Deep House, Funky, Grime—basically all the music I like to listen to when I skate. My DMs were filled with love from people new to speed skating—they loved it.

Weeks after the festival, I was still getting beautiful messages from skaters thanking me for introducing them to the UK skate scene (music and speed backward skating). I spoke with SkateLove Founder, Michelle, about the euphoric of speed skating and the London skate scene, which she was fully aware of. Now, for the first time in SkateLove's history, they are now including a speed skate showcase and speed skate masterclasses. No doubt we'll have a speed skate session on the rink, too!

I'm not DJing at the next one and I'm happy to see a whole new lineup of DJs and skate teachers. It's such a great platform for skaters old and new and I'm so grateful to have DJd two years in a row, and to introduce the London skate culture on the rink. I'd added retreats, festivals and luxury bookings and locations to my vision board, and straight after SkateLove, I was doing vision board and DJ sessions in Ibiza at a six-star luxury resort with fellow skaters. My dream is to help other skaters and creatives to manifest their absolute dream jobs and bookings and at the retreat. Celine from @HoopItOut realized and manifested her absolute dream job after our one-on-one talk about her vision. Helping people manifest their Vision2Reality is what I do as another side business (@Quest4SuccessUK).

I was booked to DJ for the very promotions and crews I loved skating with in 2022. Kai from Fix8 booked me for International Women's Day for Fix8, and later booked me for Flippers, where I was the opening DJ for the new Dr Dre Roller skates and Flippers London launch. I met Kevin Ward who said my set was the talk of their meeting the next day and that I'd gone on too early, and Liberty Ross who said it was her favorite set. Again I had branched out and played JB in addition to my usual Amapiano sounds. It was the first time I didn't skate and DJ but I still had a wicked time on the decks and it gave me the push to continue doing exactly what I do, the way I do it (I'm quite an energetic DJ and hype on the mic). I'm now one of the resident and community DJs at Flippers London playing on a regular basis. It's open Wednesday through Sunday and the general public and skate community are in love with the venue, nicknamed "The Palace". I had no idea I was the only DJ that DJs on skates (for the majority of my bookings) and my sets progressed to other genres only in 2022, my thought process being "If no one else is playing JB beats tonight (rare here in the UK and Europe), at least I've played and skated to it on my set!" I've DJ'd at skate events numerous times in Ireland, Portugal, Spain and France for FlaneurZ who have recently been added to my vision board. I unfortunately had to turn down a huge event in America due to not having the vaccine, but all systems are all go now, and I can't wait to make my debut there soon!

Rookie skates have sponsored me with a range of skates which I hire out when I DJ or teach. Rookie artistic (although now discontinued) is the staple skate for many of us jammers in the London community. We then progress on to Riedell's, and the brave few purchased Edea skates, but my broad foot rebuked that path. Having met @Gingerskates—the go to Riedell skate supplier here in Europe. I decided to support and invest with them and I adore my Riedell 336s. I went with the Arius plate thanks to the advice of SkaterDredd—our go-to skate converter here in London.

In addition to working with my favorite brands, I've been approached by organizations who provide funding for skate events and was asked to coach Storm Skater on how to skate. Meeting her in Hyde Park and seeing her teach so many people skate skills, I wanted to give back to the community and provided her with a skill which can enhance her career as a skater should she follow through. We had conversations about manifesting and positive thinking, and the opportunity came at exactly that time. We really do have the ability to speak things in to existence, it's so important to speak positively.

Prior to lockdown, I had long left the plantation and was pursuing my purpose as a life coach to assist others in transforming their vision to reality through the power of positive thoughts and actions using vision boards. I'm so happy I could practice what I preach and use vision boards to facilitate my Skate DJ dreams in such a short space of time. I've now been helping skaters to create portfolios to highlight their skills and expertise, in order to get clearer, get booked and, most importantly get paid! Many are exploited for their talents but fortunately, creatives like Hakim and Reena have created spaces to walk people through best practices, in addition to the skate classes they run weekly as Unique Flow. I invested in skate classes with Land Shark, Storm Skater, Chop & Shuffle, Wum Sum, and the one and only Sourgrapism – UKs fav jam skater.

Although I'm not a strong or advanced skater, I'm a natural teacher, previously teaching social media at London Southbank

University. Teaching adults and kids with autism, ADHD, visual and hearing impairments to DJ means I have to understand how brains tick on a whole different level. When it comes to teaching skating and jam fundamentals, I've loved seeing the progress and belief in my students. From starting off teaching eight-week skate classes with Ruthless skating (Roller derby school) to running international beginner jam sessions with skate DJ bookings. The dream is to teach these communities how to DJ so we have a collective of communities worldwide that can skate and DJ for skaters. People don't realize how important the music is in the skate scene. They go hand in hand and there's an art to DJing for sure.

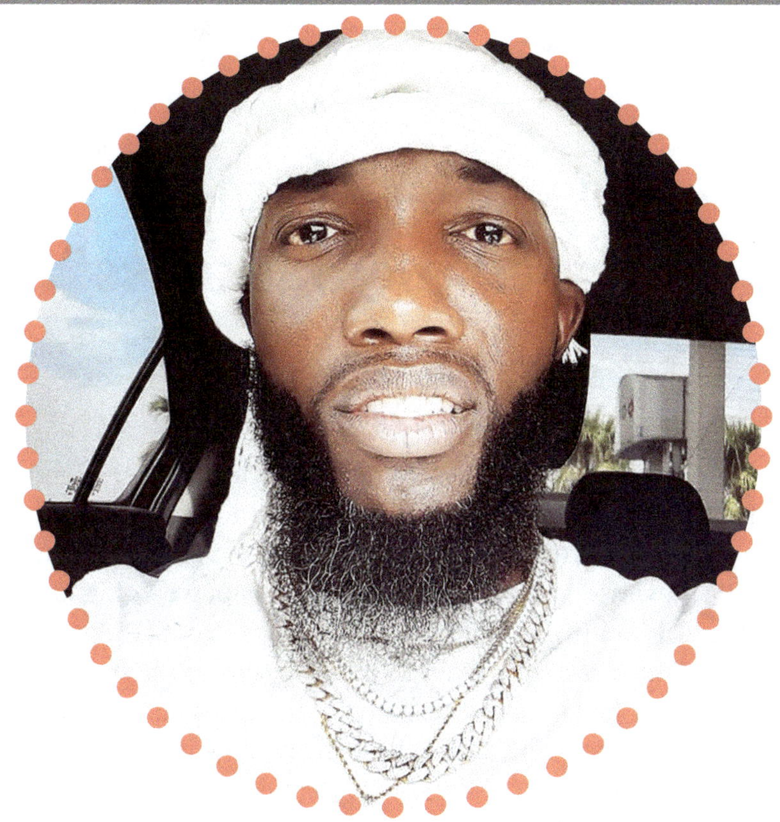

William Tate

aka Flame

Facebook: @Flame Tate | Instagram: @flameon85

"A Warrior Who Survived the Darkness"

Born in Little Rock, Arkansas, where life wasn't peaches and cream, in a community where it was very easy to get in trouble but very hard to get out, my youthful years were dark, with a dismal outlook for young Black warriors like me. My family was not well off and my three siblings and I had to grow up fast. There wasn't much positivity. My living situation was bad; I lived in a house with no lights and food at times and never had the most up-to-date clothes. This was because my mother was on drugs. She did the best she could with what she had, but the drugs won over her children and we suffered because of this. She was a single parent who didn't have much guidance in her life. At some point, when it got really bad, we were parceled out separately to other family members' homes to live until they were no longer able to care for us. My sister and I were then placed in foster care, or as they say, a ward of the state. Department of Human Services (DHS) became our parents, we were in the system. I was eleven years old at the time and I lived with one foster family until I aged out of the system. The family was nice, but it wasn't mine. I would talk to other foster kids and they told tales of being placed in homes where they were raped or beaten. I was glad I was placed in a decent home. At eighteen, I moved into my first apartment. I got a job, too. I worked at Backyard Burgers—best burgers in town. I was a cashier and the mascot, which was a rooster. Yes, that was me holding and flipping the sign on the corner when you walked or rode by. After that, I found a job at Cracker Barrel. There I was, a dishwasher/busboy. As time passed, I found a better job at FedEx

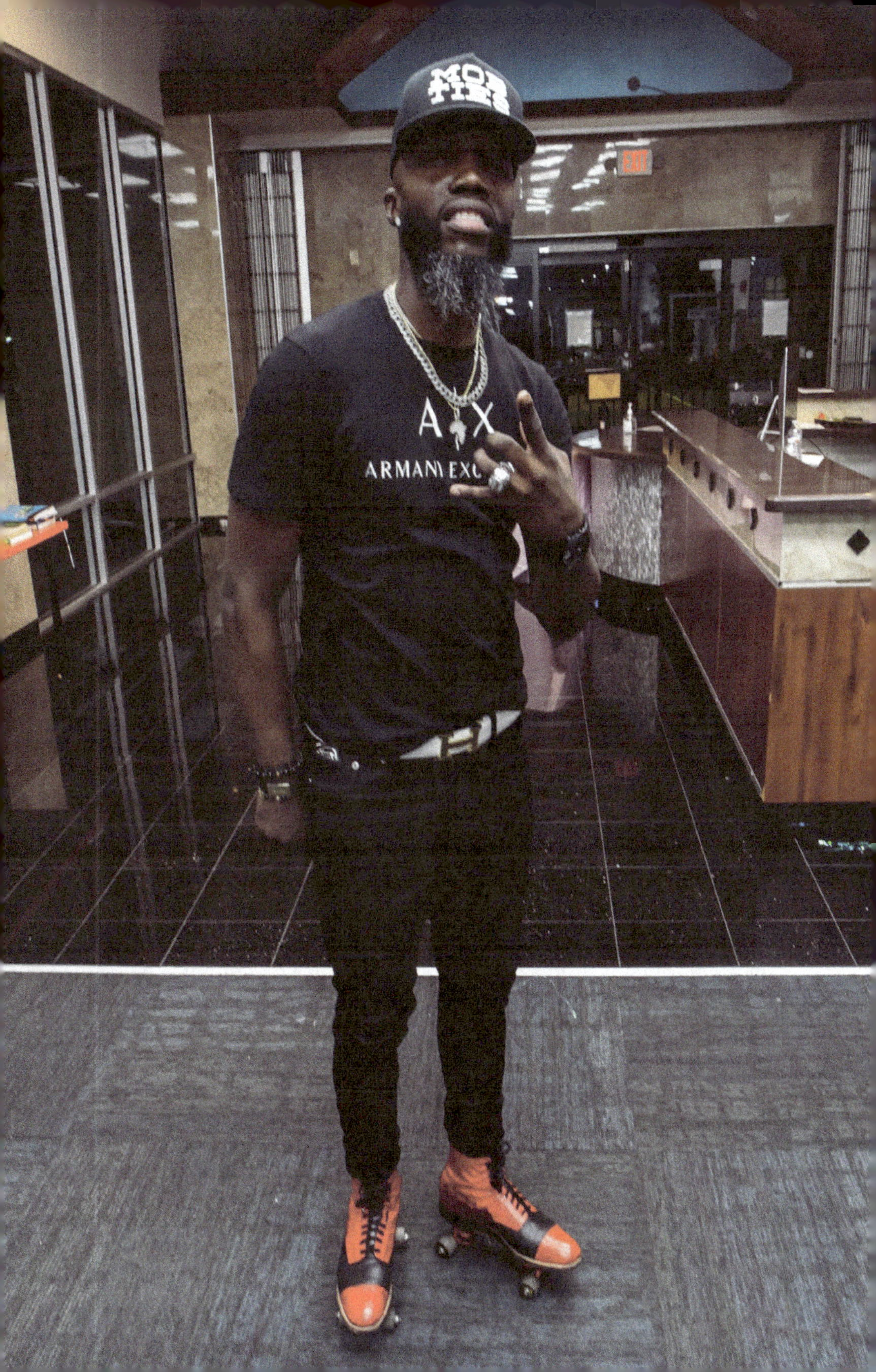
MOB
TIES
EXIT
A X
ARMANI EXC

and then I landed a job as an event specialist, which allowed me to travel and that was what I needed.

My sister enlisted in the military as soon as she was able. When she returned home, she pulled me out of the streets and into the rink. While I was working decent jobs, I had one foot in the streets and was heading down a dark hole. My sister had always been an avid skater before she left for the military and knew she had to save me from the streets and myself. She used to make t-shirts and vend them and other items at the rink. I was too young to actually be in the session, but she would take me in as her helper and I would sit at the table and watch her merchandise when she would go out on the skate floor. I would always watch her skate, and I was in awe. One day I told her, "I think I can do this." She looked at me and said, "If you wanna roll, you have to get you some skates." Say less. I scraped up the money and purchased combat boot roller skates from eBay. The wheels I had on the skates were really wide. The next time we went to the rink, I knew it would be my time to skate. My first experience with the wood was amazing. I had watched for so long that when I got on the wood, I rolled like I had been skating all my life. I always had rhythm and balance. I was a dancer and very athletic, so skating came easy. I immediately started skating fast, kind of shaky at first, but after a few times around the rink, I had my groove.

My sister saw my love for skating and she took me to my first national party. We went to the Skillz on Wheels party in St. Louis. The age requirement to get in the rink was twenty-five and up. But as my sister was a vendor, she slid me in with her, disguised as a helper. But once I was in, I was amazed. The only rule was I couldn't just go on the floor and skate by myself. I had to skate with my sister's skate crew, "Body in Motion" or the male crew, "Hell on Wheels" and skate I did. The atmosphere in the rink was like being in a club on skates. The lines were long; the music was bumping. It was like a family reunion—like you knew the people for years, but you just met them. It was a star-studded event. We played indoor volleyball for the meet and greet. We would watch the festivities from our indoor balcony. Back then it wasn't about who was the best skater, but more comradery, rep your city. Trophies were given to the largest group.

My second trip was to the Skate-A-Thon hosted by John & Joy and we skated at Cascade. You had to get there stupid early because of the lines. It was great vibes, fun; it didn't matter the age; we were all welcome. The younger cats, like me, were required to be on our best behavior. There was a room called the Boom Boom room where you could get all the goodies: moonshine, DVDs, CDs, and exotic clothing. The room was fixed up with lighting and had its own DJ. It was exciting, to say the least.

At this point, skating balanced my insanity. I began to mature. I left Little Rock in my twenties and I traveled to San Francisco and New Jersey, and I skated in the cities where I worked as an event specialist at the local sessions. Once everything was built and we had downtime, I would reach out to people that I met from traveling and I would attend the local sessions. One of my friends in Sacramento invited me to join her to a local session at—Sun Rise Skating Rink—and while I was skating they called me to the DJ booth, saying I had a phone call. It was DJ Big Bert; I was surprised. How did he even know I was in town? He invited me to come to Fountain Valley Rink in L.A. and I made it my business to go. The sessions at Fountain Valley started early at 6:00 pm and ended at 10:00 pm. When I arrived. Big Bert welcomed me with open arms. He looked out for me, then and continues to do so to this day.

Skating showed me more love than the streets. When I was in the streets, it was misery and heartbreak, but skating brought me peace. Skating has taken me to places I never imagined and introduced me to people that have uplifted me.

The third national party I attended was held in Alabama and was called "Dogg Pound." It was held in Alabama the month of January and it was cold as fu*k! It was comprised of the more seasoned skaters getting together and networking. I was always one of the youngest people at these events. The day party was nice but when you pulled up to the rink, it was built like a castle and I was like, Oooowee, I'm finna show out. I knew what I was there for and I was gonna rep my city and show my skills—put on for my city. The floor was wood, large, and felt like you were rolling on butter.

Roller skating at a national party is like the Super Bowl. Everybody from everywhere would come to have fun and rep their city. There was no sleep. You were so excited you didn't wanna miss anything that weekend . That was the excitement of the experience.

I eventually settled in Houston, Texas. I was already a known skater. I had met Ron Caesar, coordinator of the RoundUp, in previous years while in Bama at the Dogg Pound Party in 2013 or 2014.

Over the years, our friendship grew and we would talk like brothers. We stayed in touch and saw each other at various parties. I told him of my desire to move to another place and he gave me brotherly guidance and let me know if I came to Houston, he would look out for me. My home state wasn't too far away and to top it off, I could be a part of his team on his national party called the Houston Rolling RoundUp. He saw my potential to promote events and felt I would be a good fit for the team. This was part of the reason I chose Houston.

The Houston skate community was friendly but different. The only rinks I knew in Houston were Dairy Ashford and LockWood Skating Palace. I never ventured out to other rinks. The music was different from what I was used to; It was more club music. I was also used to skating with the lights out, and in Houston, they skated with the lights on. I had to adapt, which also allowed me to grow as a skater. Houston really didn't have a style. They skate fast—truck is what they called it (flying around the rink one hundred miles an hour)—and a jam dance style (nothing that I had seen before). As part of the Round Up team, I would do my part with set up at events and as I traveled extensively for work, I would promote the party.

In 2018, I felt I had blossomed, and I wanted to spread my wings and leave the RoundUp crew. I had many ideas in my head and I wanted to go off and do my own thing and throw my own party. I had always celebrated my birthday in a big way, so I headed to L.A. and did a small party with my brother Donald and DJ Mike Smooth. In 2019, I got burned out on just attending the two rinks I knew about and I heard about a Black-owned rink—The Peoples Rink—so I went to check it out.

I asked other skaters about it and got negative reviews, but I said let me go see for myself. When I got there, they welcomed me with open arms. And the rink felt like a football stadium, but for skating—the lights, sound, fog machine, party space. It read energy. I was going there so much that I started dating the owner's daughter.

I continued to have the desire to host my own party in Houston. I continued to attend The Peoples Rink. Eventually, Reggie, the owner, extended his trust in me and told me this was my home here. So, one day I spoke with him about hosting a one-day party for my birthday. To my surprise, he said, "How about doing it for the entire weekend?" I hesitated because I had never done this on my own. Reggie explained the business aspect of hosting the event and said he would financially sponsor the event. My job was to get the people there. He told me to come up with a plan on what I wanted to see and we could talk. He allowed me to decide the time of the year, the DJs, the day party events, and the hours of the party—I laid the blueprint. I was all in; I never knew this would be a big event. The party was called the Platinum Experience. I had social connections and his financial backing. I knew this would be a success. Me and Reggie wanted something big and different, so he suggested renting a boat for the day party. This had never been done before. Reggie, the house DJ, and I rode out to Galveston to see the boat. We knew the moment we stepped on the boat, we wanted it. Reggie then decided we would lease buses to transport the skaters to and from the boat. This would be epic.

I came up with the name as I knew I needed a great one. I sat with Reggie and a few others and we threw around names, but I knew I wanted a regal name. I wanted to sell an experience—and not be compared to the Round Up. We kicked around names like golden, royal, and then it clicked—the Platinum Experience.

I chose the DJs. My first call was to Big Bert. I knew I could call him. He was an OG in the DJ game and the homie. I loved Cali and wanted to make sure they came in large numbers so I also called on my brother DJ Slydz who was just learning to DJ but I needed him so I said, "Bro, I'm putting you on my party." He said, "I'm not ready," and I told him, "You got six months." My brother helped me reach out to Mike Smooth and others. The house DJ secured TL Williams to perform, as he was an artist that we skated to and we wanted a live performer. This sealed the deal. This was going to be an event for everyone to remember.

I looked around for a host hotel and knew I wanted something close to the rink. I went to Hobby Airport and looked for places. The hotel I had my eye on wasn't even built yet, but I stopped anyway and asked when they would open. I was told the spring. This would be open just in time for our event. I spoke with management and told them we were hosting a skating event and they were excited and welcoming. They spoke with corporate, called me back and we booked the spot. Ron taught me how to handle this part of securing a good location and price. I handled this like a boss.

Texas was already known for a national party, so I wanted to ensure this event would stand on its own. On the day of the event, I remember it like it was yesterday. The skaters were so excited, and I was elated to see the line of people at the door. This touched my heart and to see them show up in large numbers was a mind-blowing experience. The nights went off seamlessly and the boat experience was legendary. I wanted to do something different, and I did. We wanted to do a Platinum 2 but Covid-19 hit and, as you know, the world shut down.

During Covid-19, the rinks were under occupancy restrictions here in Texas and in many states, the rinks were closed. I found a rink in Deer Park called Skate World Deer Park. I went to the rink and spoke with the owner as I wanted to host a glow party to keep the community skating. The event was a joint venture, and that, too, was well received and a success and release for the skate community.

In the past, I had done birthday skate pop-ups in various locations, but some of my family couldn't attend, so I wanted to do something close to home. After hosting the Platinum Experience and glow party, and seeing their success, I wanted to host my own national event, and Flamez Sk8 Bash Xplosion was born. I chose the name to label the party as my own and to encompass my energy. When you see me, I am smiling and when I am on the floor, my energy is explosive. I hosted the first Bash on the Fourth of July weekend; it was a success. The next year, I duplicated the same energy with Bash number two but I moved the date to the second weekend of July on my actual birthday weekend. This invigorated me to know that I could continue to do this on my own. I used my imagination to implement things that were different. The skaters continued to support me and asked are you doing your party next year. This was humbling to know that my event was known and wanted. I always wanted to stay in my own lane. I never got in the game of promoting skate parties to compete with or go against anyone.

I got in the game to bring a new, fresh, and different approach to skate parties and the culture To expose skaters to something other than what they were used to.

It's 2023 and I am now hosting my third annual skate party. I knew this one had to be taken up a notch, and I had to bring something unique. So, I thought about putting a theme on it. I wanted to expose skaters coming this year to the city of Houston. So, I moved my party to the Galleria area and incorporated a pool party, and themed the day party as "Sk8 Nik" a play on Freak Nik…pure genius. When I plan a party, I think of the things that entice me when I attend the parties of others and I try to add the events that excite.

To sum things up, back when I was a youth, I grew up in a small city where there was very little opportunity. We had one skating rink, two malls, and the neighborhoods I frequented were hood or ghetto, as they call it. I was easily influenced not having my mom or dad to guide me. I wanted attention and love and I turned to the streets to find it. I was a hothead; I got in fights all the time. I was gang affiliated; I sold drugs and guns and was exposed to violence every day. This was why my sister felt the need to come and pull me out. My sister saved me by taking me skating. Her guidance away from the streets allowed me to open my eyes and mind to see there was something different. I was given a whole new outlook on life. My family had somewhat written me off by telling me I wouldn't live to see twenty-five. This, of course, was based on the life I led in the streets.

Before roller skating, life was dark for me. I was easily angered; I had so many unanswered questions about life, but when I put my feet on that wood, it was like my temporary fix. It allowed me to leave my life's problems behind. I met people who treated me like family and solidified my presence in the culture. Roller skating allowed me to release the built-up anger, frustration, neglect, and hurt that I had endured as a child. Roller skating brought life back into me. Before I felt like a crash dummy. I didn't care about my life, but my sister believed in me and did the best she could to get me out of the street scenes by bringing me into the rink, and for this, I am forever grateful.

Just remember, behind every smile, there is a story. I smile because I made it out. I'm still battling; the war is won but we are still in battle.

I overcame darkness, but I still have to work to maintain the light that I seek. Roller skating helps me with my mental health. Counseling doesn't work for everyone, but putting on my skates allows me to escape, even if it's just for a few hours. I can let go and not have a worry in the world.

To those battling mental health or other life situations, I say to you: even though times may be tough, never say "I can't do this." Always tell yourself that you can conquer this, you can win. Your darkest times are your most powerful moments. Take your dark energy and turn it into something positive and you can succeed. Look at me. My family had written me off at not making it to see twenty-five, but I am here and still standing and if God says the same on July 7, 2023, I will be thirty-eight years old.

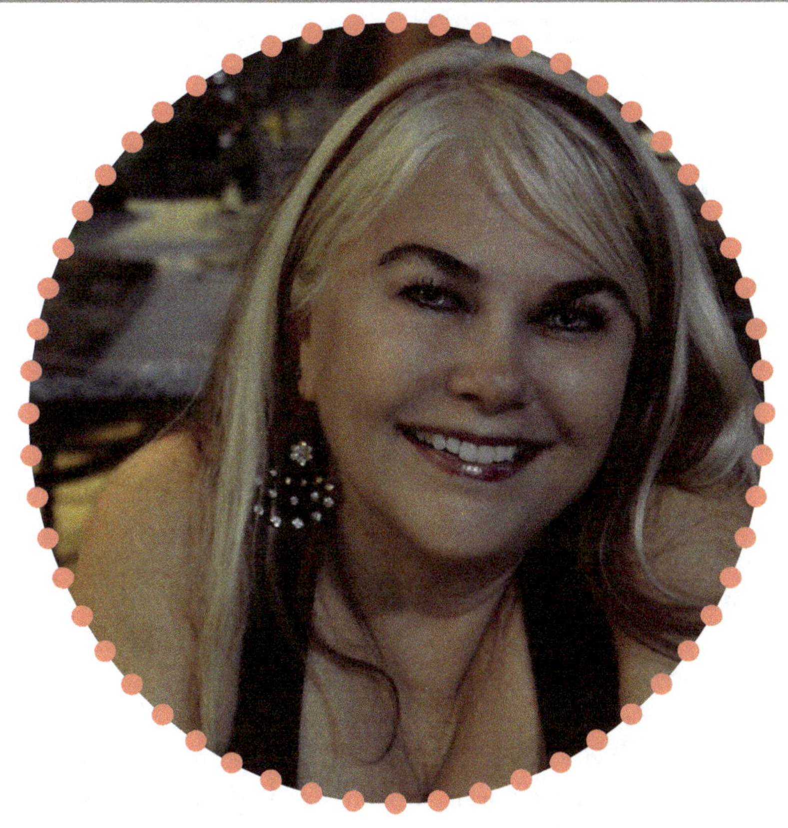

Belinda Dennis-Johnson

aka Lady B

Facebook: @Belinda Marie | Instagram: @innervisions07

"A Skating Love Story"

Where do I begin
To tell the story of a skating addiction
The sweet love story of a world that used to be
The simple truth about the life it brought to me
Where do I start?

I began skating in 1978. At twenty-three years old, I had just finished my Bachelor's Degree at UC Santa Barbara in '77 and my student teaching at UC Irvine. During this time in my life, I didn't know that I was looking for a new passion. My sister begged me to go with her to the local rink's adult night for about six months...Cypress Skateway.

I remember clearly saying, "No, skating is for kids!"

Finally, I reluctantly decided to try it. "Just once," I thought!

With its first hello
Skating gave meaning to an empty world of mine
There'd never be another love, another time
It came into my world and made the living fine
It filled my heart

I remember the feeling of exhilaration taking my first lap around the rink. I said to myself, "I will never walk again!" It felt as natural, sensual, and beautiful—as anything!

My sister didn't skate anymore...I can blame or thank her for my addiction!

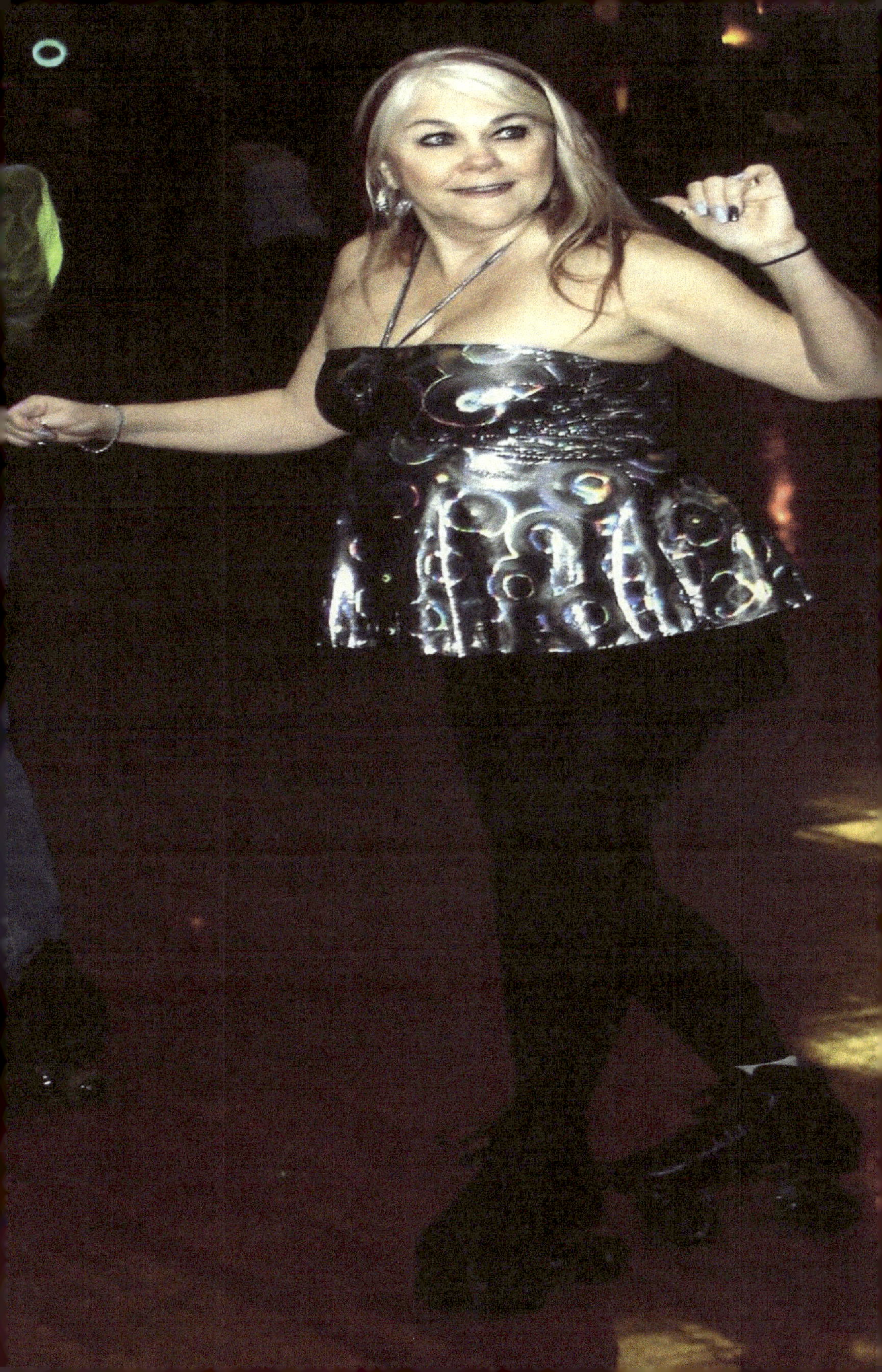

At first, I just skated around the rink, tackling backwards skating, but I knew I wanted to learn new steps, including the 'crazy legs and slingshot.' Within the first year, I began checking out other rinks…one or two adult nights per week were not enough for me. I eventually tried Flippers in Hollywood. Those who skated at Flippers know that skating there was not for beginners. We packed into the venue like sardines, so tightly that if one person went down—everyone else was going down. It was one night at Flippers, a man grabbed me from behind and began to skate with me. He was so smooth and our chemistry on the floor was something I never imagined. He told me that he had seen me skate at other rinks and we quickly formed a bond. From then on Phelan Szaabo became my skating partner. We spent countless hours learning, practicing, and teaching.

He taught me to spin and told me "once you get past 'the drunks,' you will be able to spin forever."

He was right. Spinning one hundred times was nothing!

People used to ask Phelan, "How do you get that white girl to move like that?" He replied, "We just inject her with 10 CCs of soul daily!"

Skating filled my heart with very special things
With angels' songs, with wild imaginings

In 1980, I started teaching at a middle school in Irvine. My life revolved around skating. When I finished work, I would rush home to nap so that I could skate until all hours of the night and still function at work.

Back then there were skating contests. I won my first contest as a singles skater one year after I started skating at the grand opening of Skate Depot in Cerritos.

Phelan informed me that we were going to become the new best skating couple around! Phelan told me about the best couple presently—Tasha and Tony—who had been skating together for years. Their couple's style focused on rexing and ours highlighted on the slingshot. The first contest we were in was The Brass Monkey Roller Showdown. We came in 2nd place to Tasha and Tony, but that was the last time we ever came in 2nd much to the chagrin of haters who often complained that our entry in contests should be illegal—because no one else had a chance against us. Part of our success was Phelan was an extremely talented tailor/seamster. Our costumes were always amazing.

Because I was spending so much time skating, I decided that I wanted to incorporate it into my teaching career. A fellow teacher taught surfing at Golden West College and put me in touch with the physical education department chair. I wrote a curriculum and a proposal to teach a skating class for college credit. I understood that if I didn't have at least thirty people in the class, it would fall into cancellation. Amazingly enough, I had sixty students!

Golden West College put out a news brief on its new class and the next thing I knew ABC news came out and did a story on me, *Roller Skating Magazine* did an article on me, the *Irvine World News* did an article. I felt like an overnight success! People from all over the United States and Canada were writing to me via *Roller Skating Magazine.*

One morning, my principal walked into my classroom and said, "Hey Dennis, here is what I've been doing with my day. Pulling down pictures of you from the boy's bathroom!"

I was scantily clad in living color skating on the beach on the front page of the *Newport Daily Pilot*. I guess it wasn't very teacher-like behavior! I later asked him why he didn't fire me?

He said, "I saw your potential as a teacher."

For the next several years Phelan and I competed in dance contests in clubs against lockers, break-dancers, and different genres of dancing. We created Roller Jazz Productions and did shows at LA Street Scenes, *Jerry Lewis Telethons*, and performed in schools. We procured a dance studio and people would flock to the dance studio to practice moves before the nightly skating sessions. I had skates on at least eight hours a day. We skated everywhere from Ventura down to San Diego, in clubs, rinks, and even at the beach on the weekend.

In 1981, Skating Plus in Irvine opened. Since I lived in Irvine, I was sure they built the rink for me! There were skating rinks everywhere and an adult night somewhere every night. Skating Plus had the best skating floor around. Irvine residents complained about the 'dark' element coming into their 'lily-white' community. Slowly skating rinks began to close...Laguna Hills Skate Palace, Mission Viejo Skateway, and Irvine Skating Plus. It was much like the story of the movie Roller Dreams. White communities complained about the 'element' in their neighborhoods, and law enforcement rolled in, and voila…it was the end of an era. On a side note, Phelan and I would often skate at Venice Beach, but the music master, (who will remain unnamed) was often angry about the attention we got and would turn the music off. We found our following at other beaches and brought our music. The skating world has many big egos!

We also experienced many doses of prejudice. One night after we performed at a club in Santa Monica, the police lit up sirens, pulling us over—and insisted on tearing my car apart to look for drugs. Black men in the car, in their mind, equated to 'there must be drugs.'

Roller Jazz Productions was hiring to promote Billy Barty's skating rink in Fullerton was a win-win for us—after we slam-dunked the contest in both couples and singles. One night we were passing out flyers at World on Wheels in Los Angeles. We asked the manager for permission to hand out the flyers and he said, "As long as you stay on the sidewalk which is public property."

There were three sidewalk exits, Phelan, another friend, and I each took an exit. The security guard came up to us and informed us that we were not allowed to pass out the flyers. We informed him that we had permission from the manager. He informed us that he was the manager of the outside and what the manager inside said was wrong. We went on about our business of passing out flyers. The next thing I knew the security guard ran up on me, put me in a headlock, and dragged me over to a pole handcuffing me to it. Thus, making an example out of me—in front of the skating rink for all to see. This rent-a-cop-brut then went inside to get the manager—and show him his captive little white girl! (Note: He didn't take either of the guys!) The manager came out and reprimanded the security guard and set me free. Traumatized, the guys took me to the local police station to report an assault. I never returned to World on Wheels until twenty years later and I still felt traumatized.

Sadly in 1984, Phelan and I ended our skating partnership. Continuing with Roller Jazz Productions, I hired the Venice Skaters to perform in various shows we still had contractual obligations with including LA Street Scenes—which was featured in the motion picture

Roller Dreams. I skated with another partner who came in from Arizona. He was a great skater, but the skating chemistry just wasn't the same.

I began branching out my performances to include dance and joined a Prince lip-syncing dance group and it just so happened that a show was MC'd by Muhammad Ali. I had an agent who was also Muhammad Ali's agent and after the show, my agent told me that Mr. Ali had invited me to come to his house. My skating career had led me to the home of Muhammad Ali in Hancock Park. The next day I found myself sitting across the desk from one of the greatest athletes of our time. He was kind and gracious. We didn't carry around cameras back then and it is one of my greatest regrets that I did not take a picture with him.

In 1985, the opportunity arose for me to dance on *Soul Train*. For the next three years, I incorporated Soul Train into my repertoire. My students would dance into the classroom on Monday mornings singing The *Soul Train* theme after they saw me on the show. I skated constantly but felt incomplete without a skating partner. Many asked me to partner with them, but no one had the skills of Phelan. He disappeared from the skating circuit.

In 1988, another fantastic opportunity to skate came up—the Super Bowl halftime show!

Cooley Jackson one of the Lockers whom I had previously competed against choreographed the show. Cooley, Caszper, and Jeffrey Daniels were street dancers who taught Michael Jackson the Moonwalk.

Performing in the halftime show was euphoria. I remember running through the tunnel, onto the field, and across the 100yds in my skates. I turned around and the field yielded to over fifty beautiful baby grand pianos and the Rockettes. There were eight discs on the field, and eight skaters lifted by local San Diego high school football players—set in motion—as we skated to Chubby Checker, the main performer. At the time I was five months pregnant with my first child. We practiced for three days before the show and on the 3rd day, the boys asked me if I was pregnant.

It was very cute when they shyly said, "We couldn't figure out why you are in such good shape, but you have a belly!"

The following weekend, I went back to record on *Soul Train* and the choreographer asked me if I was pregnant. He told me to come back again after I delivered. I never went back to dance, but I returned socially with my baby and still do *Soul Train* events on occasion including being in parades and attending reunions.

How long does it last?
Can a passion be measured by the hours in a day?
I have no answers now but this much I can say
I know my love of skating will never burn away
And my memories will always be right there
Within my heart

After the birth of my daughter, Karissa, and then two sons, DeRon and Jerrick, I seldom skated. My husband wasn't a fan of my skating career.

Because I don't let the grass grow under my feet, I decided to work on a Master's Degree in Counseling Psychology in 1992. Becoming licensed in 1999 paid off—after years of interning on the side and sitting for my written and oral exams. My life consisted of raising kids, being a football team mom, and cheerleading performances.

In 2002, after many years of an unhappy marriage, I filed for divorce and got my skates back out even though I was 47. The community welcomed me back with open arms and I was skating with quite a few of the skaters of yesteryear—who were around my age. A new style of skating had evolved, based on a step called 'downtown.' Once again, I found myself craving my life on skates and learning new steps. I have always enjoyed skating in the middle and doing routines with other skaters. Even as I began dating, I wasn't interested in spending time with anyone unless it didn't cut into my skate night!

I retired from teaching in 2010. I had already started a private practice as a psychotherapist in 2004. I named my practice InnerVisions Therapeutic Solutions (after lyrics from Lady T and Stevie Wonder) and it had grown enough for me to take early retirement. Little did I know, my practice would explode. I began spending more time growing a business once again and eventually less time skating. In the era of Black Lives Matter and as the mother of Black children, I truly appreciate the way Black culture has always welcomed me in. I have my own experiences with prejudice, but I am beyond blessed to consider people of all races my sisters and brothers.

My bonus daughter, Jasmin, who is now grown with her own family found *Roller Dreams* in May of 2020. She called me to tell me that I was in the movie. She proceeded to send me clips of a movie produced in 2017 that I knew nothing about.

In late 2019, I began beating myself up for not skating as much as I should. Deciding in favor of starting to balance my life and incorporate skating more—the virus known as COVID-19 struck. Will we ever be able to enjoy the golden moments in a skating rink again? I don't know, but my passion for skating will never die.

How long does it last
Can skate life be measured by the hours we have rolled
I have no answers now but this much I can say
I know I'll need to skate 'till the stars all burn away
And if there is a rink, I will be there!

Did You Know...

Maintaining Your Roller Skate

To keep your roller skates in top condition and ensure a safe and enjoyable skating experience, regular maintenance is essential. Start by inspecting all bolts and screws on your skates to ensure they are tight and secure. It's important to clean your bearings regularly to remove dirt and debris that can hinder their performance. Additionally, inspect your skate wheels for signs of wear and tear, replacing any damaged wheels promptly to maintain optimal grip and stability. Don't forget to check your toe stops and brakes for wear and tear, replacing them as needed to ensure effective stopping power. After each skating session, take the time to wipe down your skate boots to remove dirt and moisture, allowing them to air dry completely to prevent mold and bacteria growth. Lastly, make sure to periodically adjust the fit of your skates for comfort and support. By following these maintenance tips, you can prolong the lifespan of your roller skates and enjoy a smooth and safe skating experience every time.

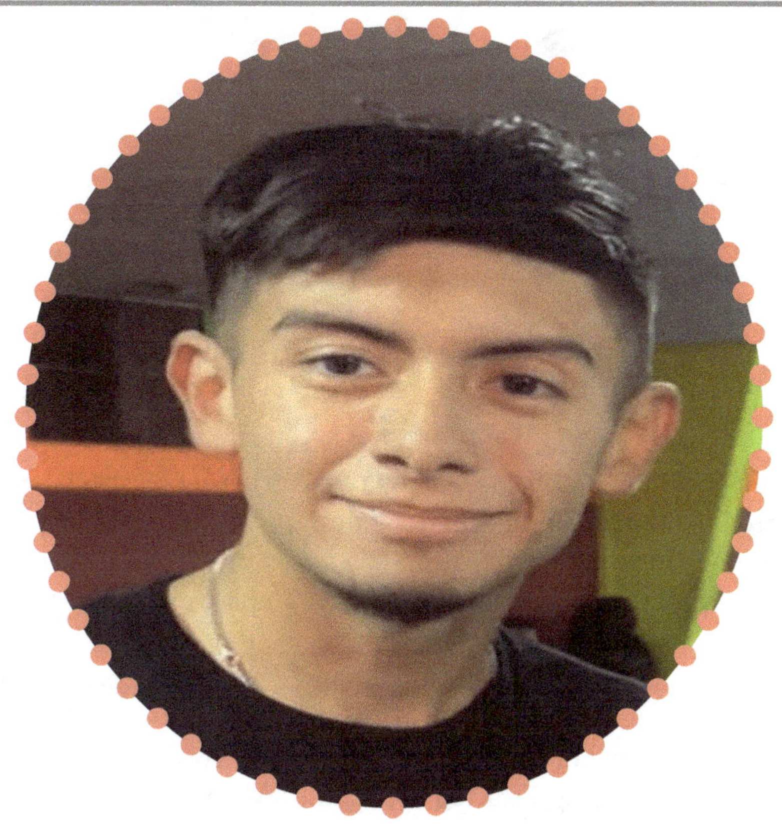

Manuel Prieto-Mejia

aka Manny

Facebook: @Manuel Prieto-Mejia | Instagram: mannythe_skater

“Unorthodox Beginning”

If you think I’m crazy, you are probably right, but I prefer being called unorthodox. My story isn’t really that intriguing or special. Skating has brought me to appreciate many things in my life and helps me to destress. I can’t really say skating has saved my life or kept me away from things, but it definitely made a huge impact on my physique and who I am.

I started skating on my birthday: June 24 (I’m a Cancer if you are wondering). I went skating just because a friend of mine invited me to go after my birthday party. I went skating a few times after that as a weekend type of thing. I started with blades. My main thing during that time was speed. Skate fast, win races, and get free drinks. These drinks were the prizes for winning the races. I put my foot into shuffle skating blades when a few of my friends started doing it themselves. There were a few of us shuffle skating in blades, but it was mainly quads.

I went to adult nights after I started working at the rink. I started working at the rink since I would go there so often; I figured I might as well work there. It was a new experience. I saw many different styles of skating but never really tried any of them. I fully started taking skating seriously after I went to the Dog Pound skate party in Huntsville, Alabama in 2020. I started wanting to travel more and go to adult nights.

Then the worst thing possible happened, Covid-19 struck. My mom had already established herself and moved to Murfreesboro, Tennessee. I later moved that summer to stay with her, along with a friend of mine. During this time, we would skate outside and just mess

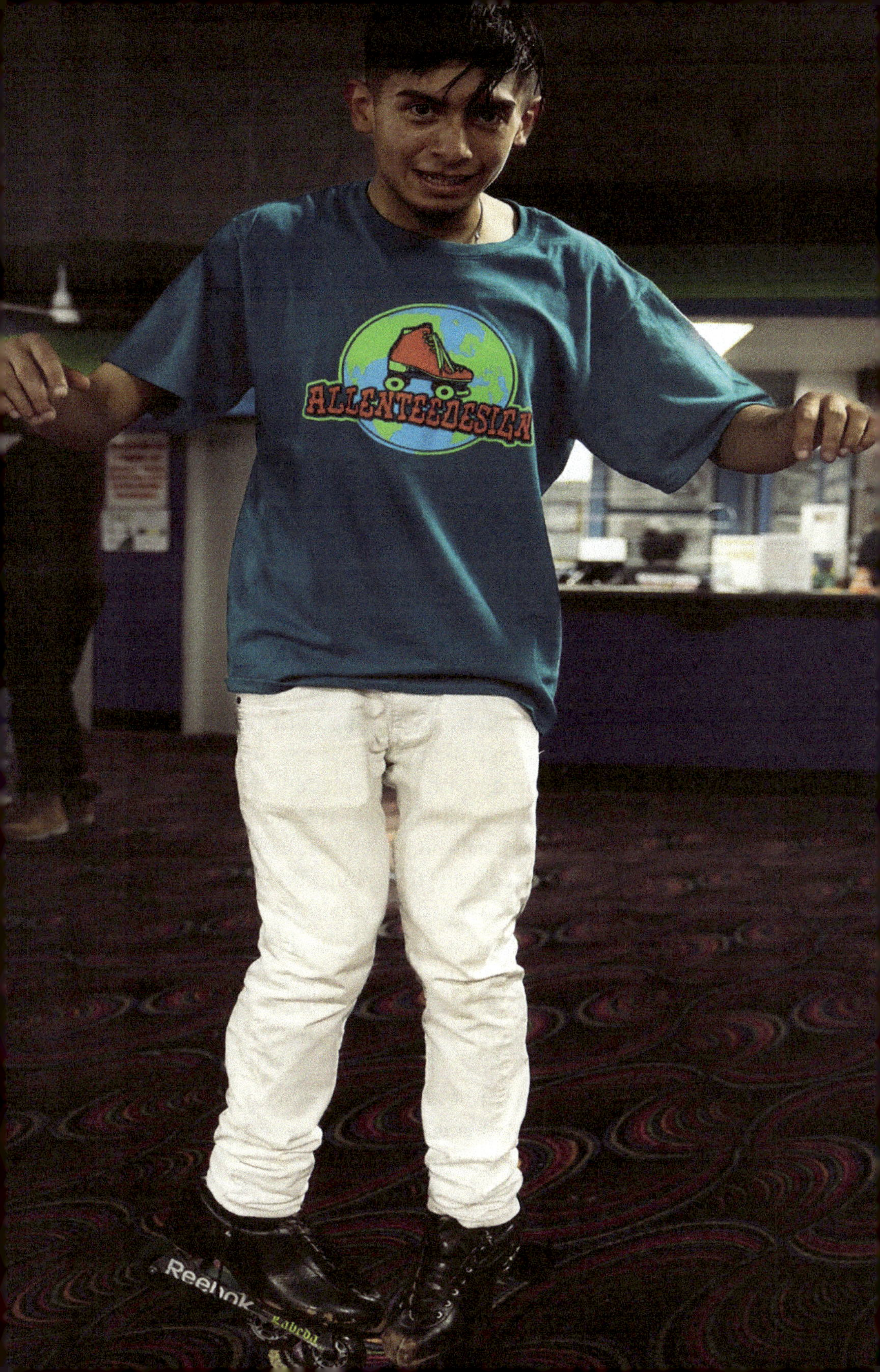
ALLENTEEDESIGN
Reebok

around. One day, he decided to visit Chris Nelson (dreamskates_by_chris on Instagram), and buy myself new skates. During this time, I got to meet and be close to the Nelson family. While purchasing skates with Chris, it was brought up that I should buy myself some quads.

At first, I was reluctant, however after discussing it with Chris and my friend, I bought some quads. After doing so, we went to the rink, and I tried out my quads. I could easily skate in them like a normal skater, but nothing too crazy. I eventually came to the conclusion that quads were too slow for me and blades were an "issue" (according to people at my local rink) to jam skate in, so I had an idea. What if I combine them? I put a blade on my right and a quad on my left. I started struggling a little however, I liked the challenge. This had officially become my new style.

A few disclaimers since these are common questions: "Do you switch sides?" No, I cannot. "Aren't you scared to hurt yourself?" I honestly don't even think about it. "How do you do it?" I honestly don't know. "Does it feel weird?" I honestly don't even feel it anymore, but it was a little weird at first.

The honest difference between skating with two different skates has to be the balance between them. I have more control over my quad and do most of my spinning with it. My blade is more for movement and speed. These two combinations help me with JB (James Brown aka Chicago-style skating), ballroom, dipping, freestyle, snapping, fast backward, and pretty much everything but middle work or anything routine. For JB, my skate style isn't as fluid or smooth as Pooh or Malik (well-known skaters who are excellent JB skaters), but it's more freestyle JB. Ballroom is one of my favorite styles. My ballroom isn't St. Louis ballroom but a variation that has been dubbed Manny ballroom. The way I do ballroom includes more of a Hispanic twist, in a sense. My blades/quad mixture makes the stopping and changing motion easier since my blade does not lose grip as quickly. Fast backward is another big one for me. My blade helps with the speed while my quad controls the direction and movement.

As I continued my skate journey, major figures influenced my skate life, Juju (juju4uu) and Kimo (whoa_kimosabe22). I grew up with Kimo's family, in a sense. I went to school with his sister, started skating with them, and met with the fam from time to time. Kimo was a role model for me when it came to skating. He made me aspire to skate with further passion. Juju brought me out of my shell when it came to skating and skate parties. My first event out of town that he took me to was Ajax, and it really exposed me to skate culture. Ajax is a trip to Atlanta, Georgia. This trip gave me my first viral video within the skate community. This video became my ticket to being recognized within the skate community. I would like to thank Terry (sk8luv33) for recording that amazing video. This video became the start of my iconic image of me with a fedora and my half and halves. Furthermore, I would like to thank two more people who, if they hadn't arrived in life, probably wouldn't be skating now. These two friends are Mitchell (mwc.jr) and Brandon (bp_loiue_13). If they hadn't entered my life a year ago, I would have reached a point where skating became boring and lost its spark. They made skating fun for me again. Skating was filled with drama and competition. When Brandon and Mitchell started skating, there wasn't any drama. It was always a new adventure, experience, and something fresh. These two have pushed forward as much as I have pushed them. They have so much potential when it comes to skating, it's insane. I appreciate them with everything I have.

Skating has allowed me to meet amazing new people, to learn different things and cultures. It also helped me start traveling more to explore and discover more about myself. A few places I have visited during my skate time are Chicago, Illinois, Atlanta, Georgia, Murfreesboro, Tennessee, Nashville, Tennessee, Birmingham, Alabama, Huntsville, Alabama, Newport News, Virginia, Lexington, South Carolina, St. Louis, Missouri, Dallas, Texas, Houston, Texas, Orlando, Florida, Tampa, Florida, Fort Lauderdale, Florida, and Toronto, Canada. My favorite place to skate would honestly have to be Sparkles off Smyrna. A large lesson I learned from my skate trips is "Money makes enemies quickly." This lesson was learned when it came to making arrangements for traveling. When it comes to traveling, you better be able to cover your own expenses and if you don't have the money, do not go. I'm also the type of person that wants to leave at a certain time so we can at least make it within a decent amount of time to rest. I do not like waiting on you to pack at the last minute, changing your mind about things last minute, or taking you shopping last minute because you forgot something with plenty of time. My honest biggest pet peeve is time. I'm not a stickler for time management, but I like to have things organized so I can optimize them as best I can.

An interesting thing about me would probably be my bearded dragons. I've always liked dragons growing up. These were the closest things to dragons, but my mom would never get one as a kid. On my birthday last year (2022), I bought them. They are my babies, and I have had them for no more than a year. I honestly take better care of them than I take care of my health. Another fact would be that I'm a workaholic. I'm always doing something throughout the day. I'm always either at the gym, work, college, or at the rink. I mainly go to the house to take care of my dragons and sleep. A future goal I have in mind is a simple mastery of each skate style. I want to blend each style and further evolve my style. Something I want to leave everyone with is: "What people think doesn't matter, just do what makes you proud and keep pushing forward."

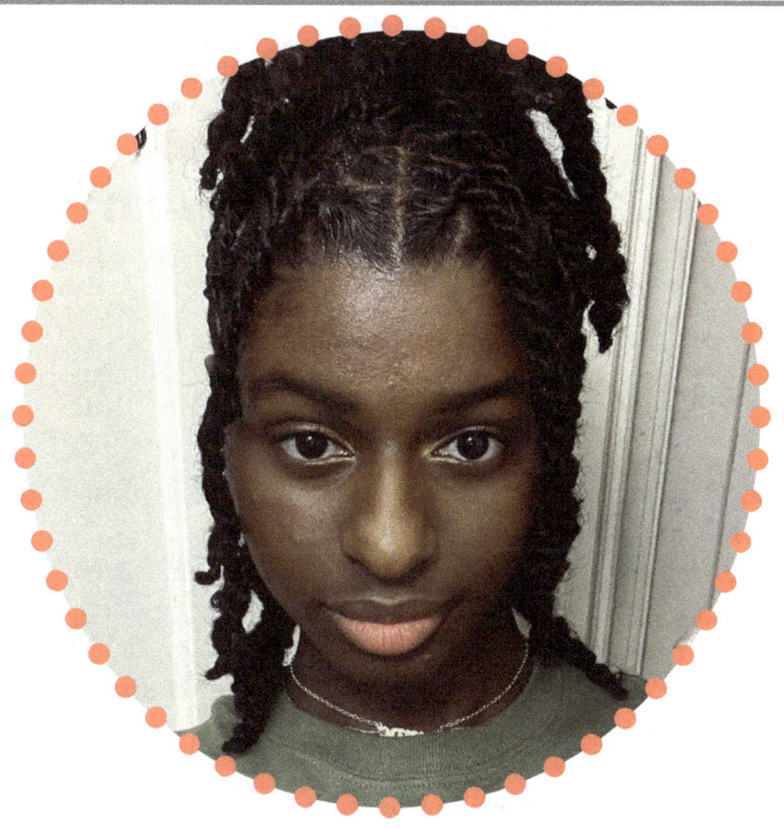

Tempest Hall

aka Tempest Nicole

Facebook: @Tempest Hall | Instagram: @Tempestnicole

"Skating is Who I Am"

Skating is who I am. It's my escape from the real world. It changed my life.

My name is Temptest Hall aka Temptest Nicole. I'm currently twenty-seven years old, a mother of three—born and raised in Cleveland, Ohio.

When I was a kid, our school would take us on field trips to the rink. During the week in school, we would get coupons for a local skating rink named Zelma George (United Skates). At the time my mom would take us there and my oldest brother would have to hold my hand because I didn't know how to skate. My brother hated it because our wheels would connect causing a fall. As soon as we fell, a floor guard would make us go to the (beginner's/cool-down area) middle circle—which added to my determination in learning how not to fall! That way, my brother's trips to the middle wouldn't have to involve me.

When I was a teenager, Friday nights were 'teen nights' at Zelma. I would go as often as I was able to with my friends—but I couldn't always get rentals because my mom would only send me with the admission money. Having eight other siblings helped my understanding that she did not have the extra money for me sometimes, plus it wouldn't be fair to the rest of my siblings. So, I would just be there hanging out with my friends—which also worked! I was (still am) in love with R&B music—but at the rink—they only allowed backward rink-flow and a couple of skaters on the floor. With my not knowing how to skate in the reverse fashion—I had to sing along and watch. My way of stopping was to skate to the rails or wall to stop myself. We even had a church

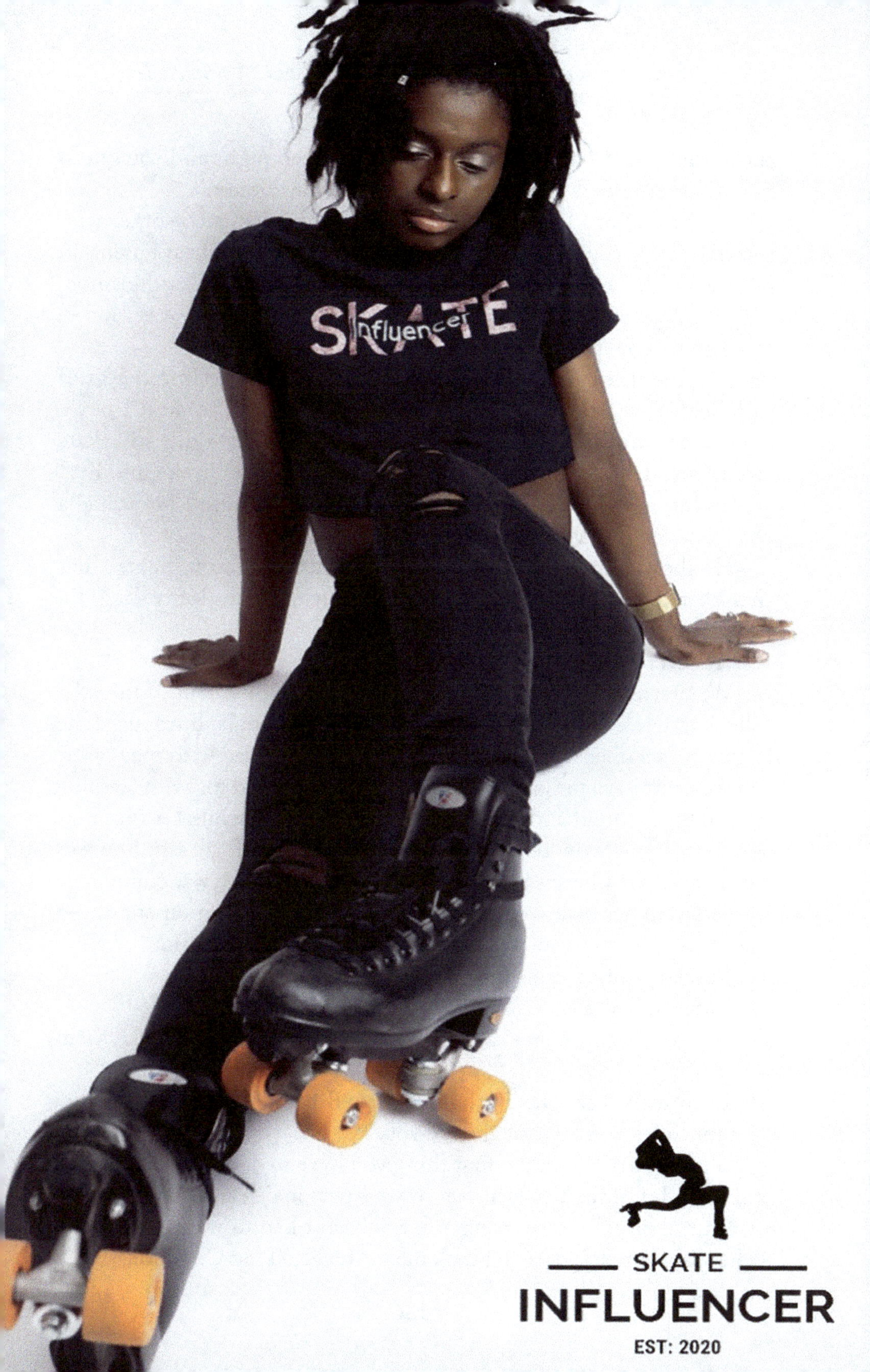
SKATE
Influencer
SKATE
INFLUENCER
EST: 2020

called the 'The Word Church' that offered a teen night and you got in free if you attended the 'teen church' before the session.

At the end of December 2015, as an adult, I had a coworker who was like my best friend—his name was Jai. He would always mention how he wanted to go skating because he just needed to clear his mind.

One day I said, "Let's go skating! I haven't been since I was a kid—but I know how not to fall."

Jai, I, and a couple of other coworkers went to United Skates of Wickliffe for the adult night which shocked me because I never knew there was such thing as an adult night and that adults still skate constantly as we did when we were teens. While I was in the middle, I was trying to figure out how to skate backward because I never had a chance to learn it as a kid, so I asked Jai to show me.

He showed me how to position my feet and the movements—but then skated away when the song changed saying, "This is my song! I'll be back."

Jai never came back.

We started going to Pla-Mor Roller Rink in Euclid, Ohio the following week to their family sessions. This is where Jai introduced me to two girls named Lexi and Sammi. Both girls skated with me before, so I wouldn't have to skate by myself. They also helped me with learning how to turn around and 'backwards skate.' One day while I was at Pla-Mor, I saw this woman skating so smoothly and effortlessly. She was the first female I have seen skating in the moment; she was completely immersed in her own world. Then it clicked, from that moment on—I understood what Jai meant about skating clearing his mind.

I asked Jai if he knew her, he said, "Yeah, that's Jax."

Later that session I saw Jax and her husband.

And in seeing them skate together, I said, "I want to be like them one day."

Eventually, I saw Jax in the middle and I went up to her and said, "I want to learn how to skate like you."

She replied, "Well, the first thing you have to do is get your skates, it'll feel a lot different with a set of your personal skates."

At the time I was starting a new job, so I had to wait for the new skates. In February 2016, Jai took me to "IcyHOT" in Columbus, Ohio at Skate Zone 71. When I tell you I bout lost my mind! It was gone with excitement! There were so many people there from ALL OVER! The music was bumping from outside, we parked far away because the rink parking lot was fully PACKED! The line to get in wrapped around the building. When we finally got inside, the building's situation was no different from the parking lot—IT WAS PACKED! Jai asked me if I wanted to go get some rentals skates and I told him no because I was going to be the only one there that didn't know how to skate. Plus, I had some fear about even trying to get on the floor. So, I watched the whole night from the sidelines. By the end of February, I finally got my pair of skates! To build my skills, I started going skating around five to six times a week.

I've made so many friendships through skating. Many of them are even closer than my own family. I had a skate best friend/sister named India—and our thing was splits! Every session we went to together, we performed the splits. Dating a skater led to a trip to Joi's Sk8-A-Thon in Atlanta, Georgia on Labor Day Weekend 2016. We ended up having a great time, meeting a couple of new people—and skating the nights away. Unfortunately, the short relationship didn't work out, as my skating love interest disappeared. Later on, I found out it was because of an ex and some assorted drama—so I told myself—I wouldn't date any more skaters. In this culture, and locally, I found out many of the people I am cool with—all had some sort of previous relationships. With my being new to the scene, I didn't want to have any drama in my newfound happy place. Things did not get any easier, as dating a 'non-skater' was a headache because they didn't understand how big skating was to me. Assuming I was cheating with someone at the rink always flared up issues—so those relationships never worked out either.

Fast forward to August 2019, we were doing splits at the end of a skate session and a skater recorded me and sent the video.

I posted the video on my social media and to a skate group on Facebook with a caption saying "I'm gonna split until I can't no more, so who's with me?"

India and another skater commented with their split videos. One of the skaters named Kelvin (Pooh) commented with a video of him doing a nutcracker and I replied by saying, "I like my knees."

After this exchange, we became the best of friends. He was in Texas and I was in Ohio, so we did video calls every day since then and would talk about our problems giving each other advice. Pooh mentioned his birthday coming up and that he planned on taking a week off from work. He asked me if I didn't mind him coming up to visit so we could hang out. I agreed, and he booked his flight. I showed him around Cleveland and took him to both of our rinks here—where he ended up knowing a lot of people! As it turns out, Pooh saw people he hadn't seen in forever from traveling to skating parties over the years. A couple of months later, Pooh called India and planned to come to Cleveland to surprise me by asking me to be his girlfriend. India and her boyfriend (now husband) picked Pooh up from the airport, then called my sister Ne'sha to make sure I was home—so she could let him in the house. He walked into my room with flowers and the new Call of Duty game that I wanted that just premiered. Needless to say, I accepted and we became official! The next month, I went down to Houston to visit for a date. Pooh gave me a promise ring further declaring his love.

In the summer of 2020 Pooh and January (a JB skater from Chicago but moved to Cleveland at the end of 2019) were talking about how dope it would be if they could get some JB skaters to come to Cleveland and do a JB takeover for a night. So, I suggested that we throw a birthday/welcoming party for Pooh in September since he was moving to Cleveland. We would call it 'Chicago Meets Cleveland.' Upon speaking to Miguel, the owner of Mig's Pla-Mor—he gave us the thumbs up to start planning the event. I made a save-the-date post on social media. January reached out to a couple of skate DJs in Chicago to see who would contact us back first as far as coming to Cleveland to DJ alongside DJ Iceman—who's the home disc jockey for Pla-Mor. We ended up getting a message from DJ T-Rell saying he'll come out and deejay, so we booked him.

One night, I was talking to T-Rell on the phone with Pooh and he was telling me how he couldn't wait to see my pinball split in person and I told him I wanted to see him do a helicopter split in-person. Pooh kept asking me if someone told me to stop in a certain spot—when I do the pinball—would I be able to do it? Every time I told him yes!

September 12, 2020, came and it was now Pooh's birthday and the night of his party. Midnight came so we started roll call and Cleveland went first. After Cleveland, it was Chicago's turn and whenever you go to a skate party that had a Chicago or JB call at the end they do splits and one stops. Everyone out on the floor doing their thing; we splitting then I hear T-Rell on the mic telling everyone to clear the middle and asked me to come here. T-Rell asked me to do the pinball and land right in front of Pooh so this whole time I'm thinking like okay so y'all are just going to challenge me at the party, bet, let me prove to y'all two that I can do it. So, I come around, pick up some speed and I go for the pinball split and landing right in front of Pooh.

As I turn around to tell him, "I told you so!" Pooh leaned over and said, "Will you marry me?" I was lost. Stunned. I replied, "…wait, what?"

I know he jokes around a lot, but then I see the ring in his hand and heard Let's Get Married by Jagged Edge playing in the background! Immediately, I started crying—never knowing this whole time I was planning my proposal!

If I can give any advice to any new skaters—it would be to always stay true to yourself and skate for you. There will always be haters in anything you do—but there will also be people who care for and love you as well. Focus on the positive— even when the negativity is louder. Respect others as well as differing skate styles. Learn the history and travel to different rinks. I started posting my first skating videos to try and convince my friends and family to come out and learn how to skate with me. As I got better, my Aunt Michelle would tell me to keep sharing them because she loved to watch them on Facebook. In 2019 she told me not to stop skating. Aunt Michelle told me someone needs to pay me—because I was that good of a skater! Around October 21st, 2020, my mom called and told me that my Auntie had passed away. I made sure that next skate night—I skated as if she was watching. Skating does something to spirit, it's like a natural high with exercise.

Whenever someone comes to me for advice, I'll tell them to try roller skating.

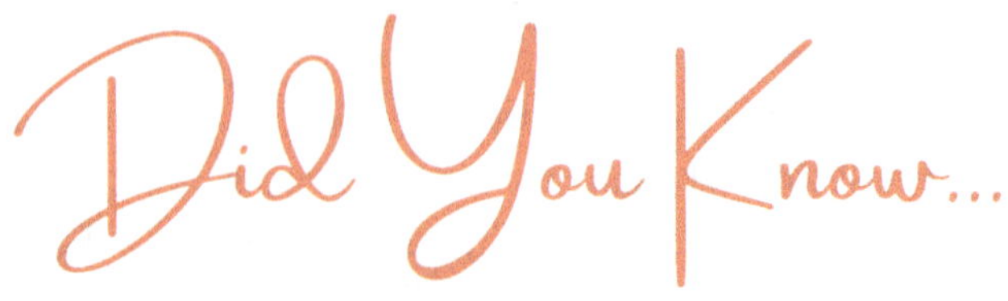

History of Skate-a-thons

Skate-a-thons are events where participants skate for an extended period, often to raise funds for charitable causes or organizations. These events typically involve individuals or teams skating for a set duration, such as several hours or even an entire day, with participants collecting pledges or donations based on the distance skated or simply as a flat contribution.

The concept of skate-a-thons has roots in the broader tradition of endurance events and charity fundraisers. While the exact origins of skate-a-thons are difficult to pinpoint, they likely emerged in the mid-20th century alongside the growing popularity of roller skating in communities across the United States.

Skate-a-thons became particularly popular during the roller skating boom of the 1970s and 1980s when roller rinks were prevalent social hubs. These events provided skaters with an opportunity to come together, showcase their skills, and support worthy causes simultaneously.

Over the years, skate-a-thons have evolved to encompass a wide range of formats and themes, from family-friendly community events to competitive endurance challenges. Some skate-a-thons are organized by roller skating clubs, schools, or community organizations, while others are held in partnership with charitable foundations or nonprofit organizations.

Regardless of their specific format or purpose, skate-a-thons continue to serve as a fun and meaningful way for skaters to contribute to their communities while enjoying their favorite pastime. Whether participants skate for personal achievement, to honor loved ones, or to support a cause they care about, skate-a-thons embody the spirit of camaraderie, philanthropy, and the joy of roller skating.

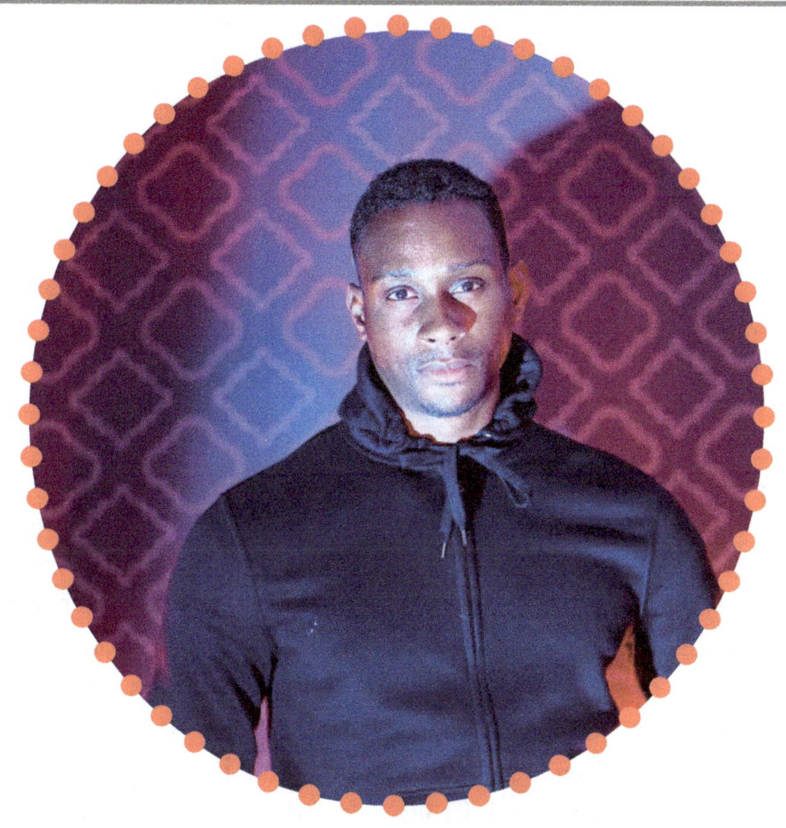

Harry Martin

aka Studio 50H

Facebook: Harry Martin | Instagram: @rollerwavenyc

"The Roller Wave"

I founded The Roller Wave after unexpectedly having the time of my life at a company party held at LeFrak Center at Lakeside Prospect Park. At the time I hadn't skated since childhood, so it felt like discovering hidden treasure. After going back night after night for an entire summer, I looked for new rinks around the boroughs hoping to find better music and possibly a crowd rooted deeper into authentic skate culture. It was then I found myself in Bed-Stuy at a Salvation Army gym turned part-time makeshift rink. The only thing lacking there was a youthful crowd. I then decided to negotiate my own skate night with the management, bringing out a bevy of promoters, speakers, DJs, and photographers. Roller Wave opened up space to a wider, more diverse audience and after a difference of opinions, I parted ways to look for a space more suitable to my vision.

I then put together a few proposals and shopped them to potential venues with the disclaimer saying, "I know this might sound crazy, but we want to turn your space into a pop-up Roller Disco."

Luckily, The House of Yes in Bushwick was crazy enough to give it a try. I rented the skates for my first event but after facing difficulties with the distributer, I decided that saving every penny of profits from all events and investing in an inventory of roller skates was a better move. Pooling my resources, which was risky at this point because I had a baby on the way—had to be done. The risk paid off in that since June of 2016, The Roller Wave has held thirty-eight sold-out events at

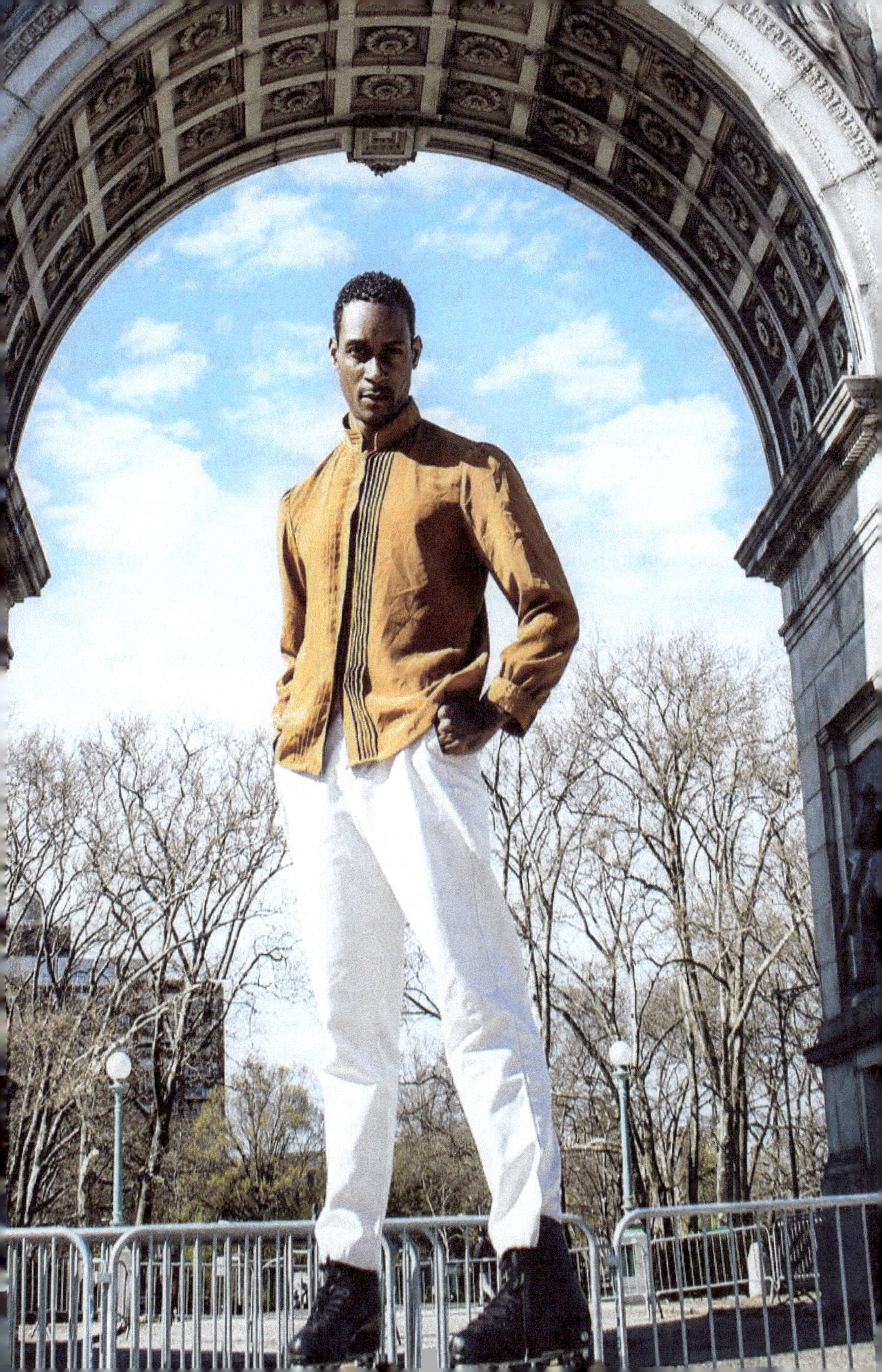

The House of Yes and has expanded to The Ludlow House in the Lower East Side, Alpha Space in Crown Heights, Gantry Loft in Long Island City, Soho House in the Meatpacking District, Tao Restaurant for Alicia Key's birthday party, The Williamsburg Hotel with Everyday People, and The Union Square Ballroom. I have even hosted celebrities such as The Bronfman's, Alicia Keys and Swizz Beatz, Mel Gibson, Michael. K. Williams, the Top 100 YouTube Influencers of 2019, and many more.

Now a father and a black small business owner, I can attribute the success of the events to my genuine passion for the culture and respect for the history of Roller Disco alongside the desire to introduce a lost art to a new generation.

I understand roller skating is not a completely lost art—but just in my experience—I have seen a lot that points my opinion in that direction.

Growing up in Crown Heights Brooklyn, I was a frequent flyer at the Empire Roller Skating Rink.

As a toddler, I used to love summer trips and or after-school trips to the rink. I was always practicing at an early age, whether it was how to skate backward, fast, or doing 180-degree jumps. By the time I became a teen, I began visiting Empire Skating Rink every Friday night for their teen night. My first couple of weeks during the teen night, my mom would only let me go if I would let my little brother tag along. Teen night first started as a great party to mingle and skate with peers, but then slowly started to turn into a dance party for teenagers.

As I grew older (fifteen or sixteen years old) pressures of fitting in with peers started to settle in. Fitting in on the streets of Brooklyn, New York in the early 2000s was more like hooking up with the opposite sex, joining street gangs, and hanging with the popular crowds. The popular crowd at the time was more into dancing and wearing the latest fashion. Skating began to die down during teen night at the skating rink (it was like you weren't cool if you were skating at the time). Teens then used the skate floor as a dance floor, which I hated but wanted to fit in, so I chose to not skate anymore.

The day I rediscovered roller skating—back in the year 2015—came at a time when I still to this day, say it was the lowest point of my life. In my late twenties, I felt like life had no direction. Before that event at Le Frak center, I was battling deep depression. I felt like giving up on everything in life, I had no ambitions or cared for myself. During the time, I knew I was dealing with depression, so I became an avid runner. Using running as a tool to battle my depression helped— but did not fully solve the problem.

Going out to the rink every day practicing helped saved my life at the time. I began to equate roller skating to running and how it has very similar benefits but was far more fun and also healthier for the knees and other joints than running.

Roller skating became my workouts, I would spend hours getting my cardio on and enjoying old school disco, house, and funk music. I understood how roller skating impacted my life so deeply at the time, so I decided I wanted to be around peers like that to experience this same feeling.

I am currently still hosting roller discos even during the pandemic. When the pandemic started just like everyone else in the world, I began to experience, depression, fear, anxiety and became uninspired. I was scared to go outside. I sat in the house for about two months straight—afraid that I would catch the virus and die.

This feeling I had experienced before in life so I thought to myself, “I will not let this defeat me either.”

I began going to the park every day with the thought of building my immune system through fitness so that if I did get sick, I would overcome it. I will not allow anything or anyone to stop me, was my mindset. As I worked out every day in the park, I started seeing a bunch of people in the parks with roller skates. At this point, I was so happy and joyous to see all of the new skaters popping up everywhere. So, I decided to start an outdoor roller-skating series during the pandemic. As it turns out, I brought about two-hundred pairs of skates to the local park and began hosting free roller skate sessions. These outdoor skate sessions, I feel, are one of my biggest accomplishments besides starting the Roller Wave back in 2016.

There are so many testimonies of my peers telling me how it saved their lives during 2020. Just like me, they were coping with a lot of pressures from the pandemic and needed an outlet to feel free and joyous again. I am so happy that I can share my light—with the same wonderful communities I try to have an impact on!

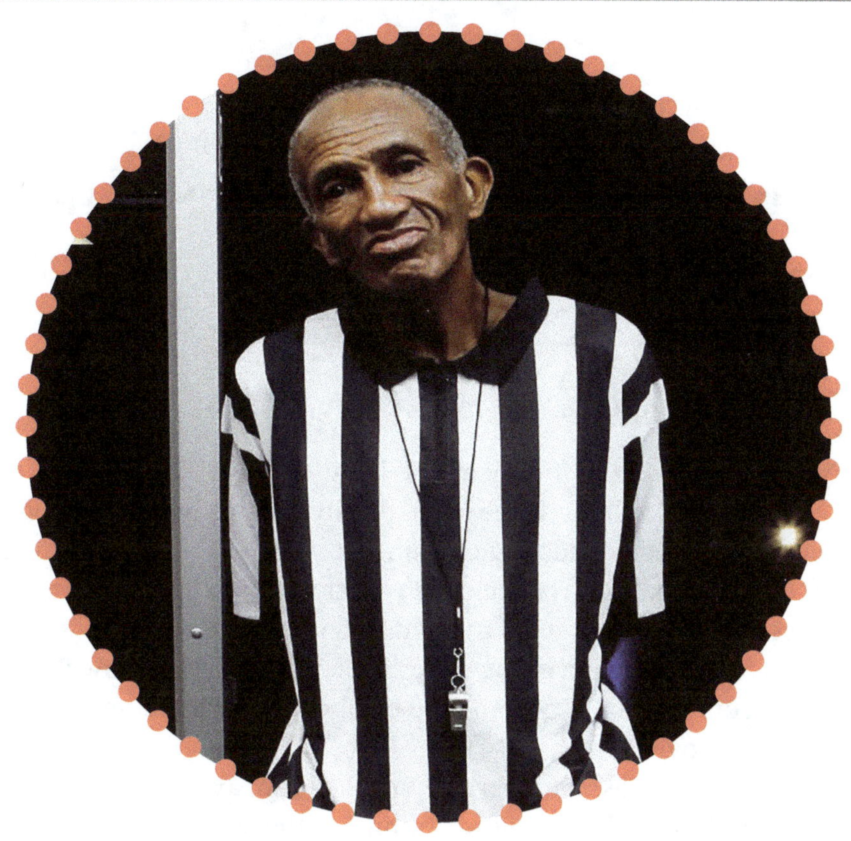

Terry Marshall

aka Jump Rope Man

Instagram: @terrymarshall969

"Unleashing Thrills On Skates"

Born and raised in the heart of New Orleans' 7th Ward, Terry Marshall, aka Jump Rope Man, discovered his innate passion for roller skating at the tender age of nine. It was during those formative years that Terry's very first memory was etched into his mind—a vivid recollection of rolling on his trusty union iron skates outside, soaking in the sheer exhilaration of the experience. Little did he know that this initial encounter would become the catalyst for an incredible journey that spanned over forty years.

Fueling his passion, Terry's mother, an avid skater herself, introduced him and his seven siblings to the world of skating at a young age. It was a family affair—a shared love for the art of gliding on wheels that brought them closer together. Terry's mother, an unwavering source of inspiration, continued to grace the rink for an astonishing seventy years, her skates spinning with grace and determination until her passing at the remarkable age of eighty-one.

An exceptional skater, Terry has earned his reputation as "Jump Rope Man" through a breathtaking display of agility and precision. His extraordinary talent lies in seamlessly combining the art of jumping rope with the fluid motion of roller skating. This distinctive fusion has garnered him widespread recognition and a devoted following.

In 2012, Terry took his performances to new heights by incorporating a mask into his act. The addition of the mask heightened the thrill of his performances, infusing an air of intrigue and mystery. Skaters were enthralled as they marveled at the seamless synchrony of

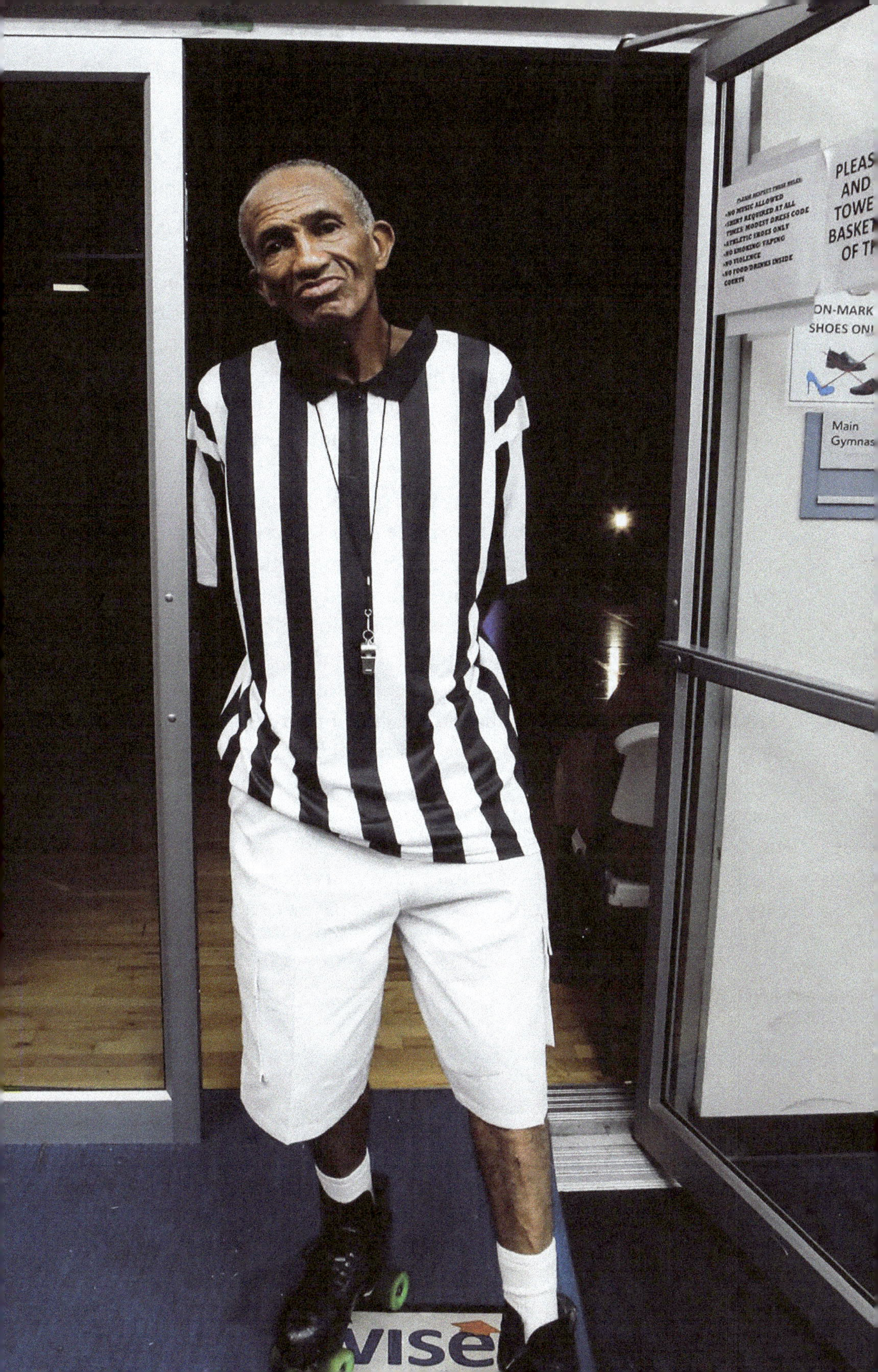

PLEASE RESPECT THESE RULES
•NO MUSIC ALLOWED
•SHIRT REQUIRED AT ALL
TIMES MODEST DRESS CODE
•ATHLETIC SHOES ONLY
•NO SMOKING/ VAPING
•NO VIOLENCE
•NO FOOD/DRINKS INSIDE
COURTS
Main
wise

Terry's jumps and spins, all while his true identity remained concealed beneath the mask. The skate community's enthusiastic response was overwhelming, as it embraced this enigmatic persona that Terry had carefully crafted.

While Terry enjoys skating in various rinks, it's the vibrant atmosphere of skate parties that truly captivate him. Among the multitude of memorable events, there are a few standout favorites that hold a special place in his heart. The Houston Rolling RoundUP, Dallas Sk8 Fair Classic, and Joi's Skate-AThon are events that Terry eagerly anticipates, joining fellow skaters to create unforgettable moments on the dance floor.

Once Terry steps foot into the rink and dons his skates, a profound transformation takes place. It is as if the outside world dissolves, and he enters a realm where nothing else matters. Any burdens or concerns that may have troubled him before are effortlessly pushed aside, replaced by a profound sense of peace and liberation. Skating becomes his sanctuary, a method of relaxation and a means to clear his mind.

Skating is not just a hobby or a fleeting interest for Terry—it is an enduring passion that has shaped his life. From the moment he first stepped onto the rink, he knew he had found his calling. It has become an integral part of his identity, woven into the fabric of his being. Terry's connection to skating runs deep, permeating every aspect of his existence.

Prepare to embark on an extraordinary adventure as the captivating story of Terry Marshall unfolds within the pages of a future volume of The Evolution of Skating.

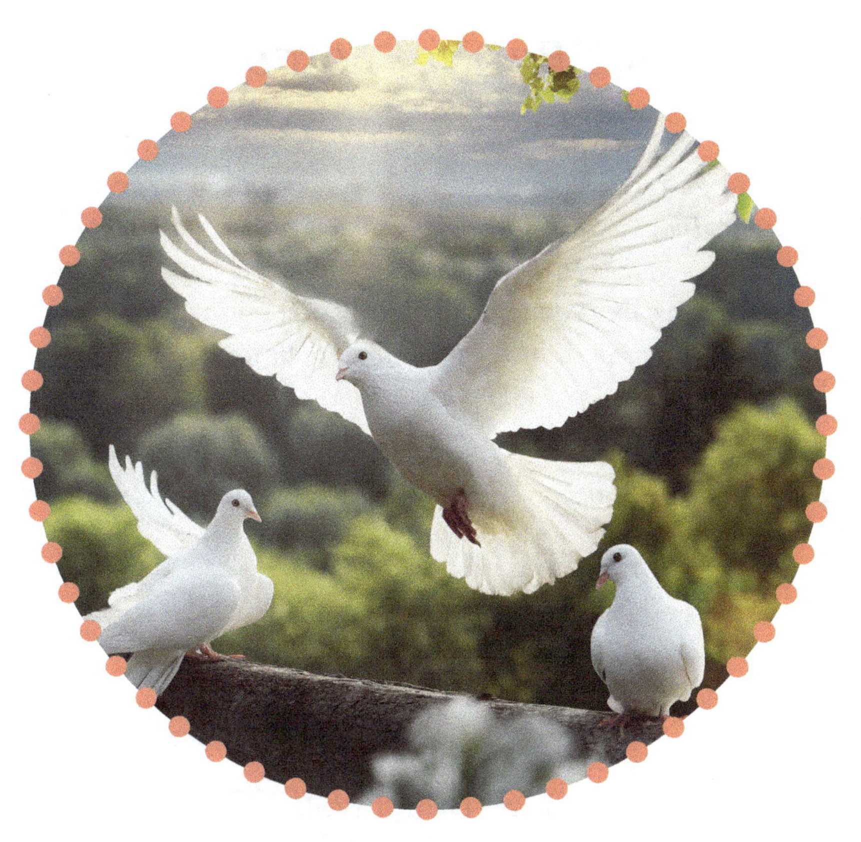

In Memoriam

"Gone But Not Forgotten"

"I know for certain that we never lose the people we love, even to death. They continue to participate in every act, thought and decision we make. Their love leaves an indelible imprint in our memories. We find comfort in knowing that our lives have been enriched by having shared their love."

–Leo Buscaglia

Sending peace and prayers to those in the skate world whom we have lost but who shall never be forgotten.

Jabarie Smith
Yancie Binkley
Kimberly J. Dent aka Kimmi D
Joseph C. Reyes Jr.
Brian "Bee" Potter
Larry Darnell Wells
Christopher Banks
Isaiah K. Isreal
Angelisa "Angel" Burgin
Romeo Moore
Josephine Smith Huyghe
Gloria Mays

For those not mentioned, you will forever be in our hearts, prayers, and in our souls with each roll of our wheels.

In Loving Memory of Kimberly J. Dent

Gone Too Soon.

By Doris Patrick
President, Virginia Skate Connection

Kimberly J. Dent was born on December 17, 1969. Also known as Kimmi D & Kim, her father preceded her in death on August 19, 1969. She was raised by me, with her older sister and brother.

OMG, Kim was an adorable baby girl. As she grew, she became our mother. She acquired a love for skating at an early age. She graduated high school. Yes, she had a curfew of midnight. On several occasions, she missed her curfew and we would have our discussion. She didn't always agree with me. This particular night she decided that it was time for her to move out. Yes, I was in shock, crushed, and in disbelief as she was packing. When you live in my home you have to abide by my rules. I always knew where she was and whom she was with; that didn't stop me from crying, praying, and worrying about her.

When living away from home she started working at Skate King in East St Louis, Illinois, in 1985 and at a hamburger restaurant, taking care of her needs. After a year she decided she wanted to return home. I was truly glad when that day arrived. I welcomed her back with much joy and happiness. The world wasn't what she thought it would be, trying to be grown.

She never lost her desire for skating. She took a break from Skate King to further her education for her new employment with the Internal Revenue Service. She returned to Skate King and worked both jobs for thirty-plus years until her passing on April 23, 2023.

At Skate King, Kim was loved, respected, and a no-nonsense individual. You either loved her or disliked her. There was no in-

between. That was how she operated there. She mentored, loved, and adopted many and was a community of beautiful people.

I am so grateful to Mr. Foggy and the skate family for their love for my daughter, Kimberly J. Dent.

Sincerely,

Doris Patrick, a proud mother

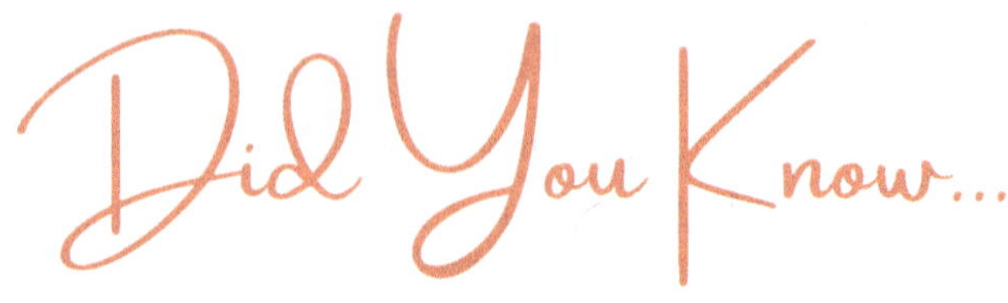

Sneaker/Shoe Skates

Shoe skates, also known as sneaker skates or shoe roller skates, have become increasingly popular among roller skating enthusiasts. This customization allows skaters to express their personal style and preferences while enjoying the activity of roller skating. By replacing the traditional boot or shoe part of roller skates with regular shoes or sneakers, skaters can showcase their unique personality through their choice of footwear.

One advantage of shoe skates is the greater comfort they provide. Skaters can use their own familiar and well-fitted shoes, which may offer better support and cushioning compared to traditional roller skate boots. This is especially beneficial for skaters who have specific footwear preferences or require specialized support for activities like skating.

Moreover, shoe skates offer a wide range of styles and aesthetics. Skaters can choose from a variety of sneakers or shoes to customize their roller skates, matching their skating gear with their personal fashion preferences. This flexibility in design adds an element of individuality and creativity to roller skating, allowing skaters to make a fashion statement on wheels.

Additionally, shoe skates provide practicality and convenience. Skaters no longer need to switch between shoes and roller skates when transitioning from regular footwear to skating, making it easier to engage in spontaneous skating sessions. This accessibility makes roller skating more enjoyable for a broader range of individuals, contributing to the growing popularity of shoe skates in the roller skating community.

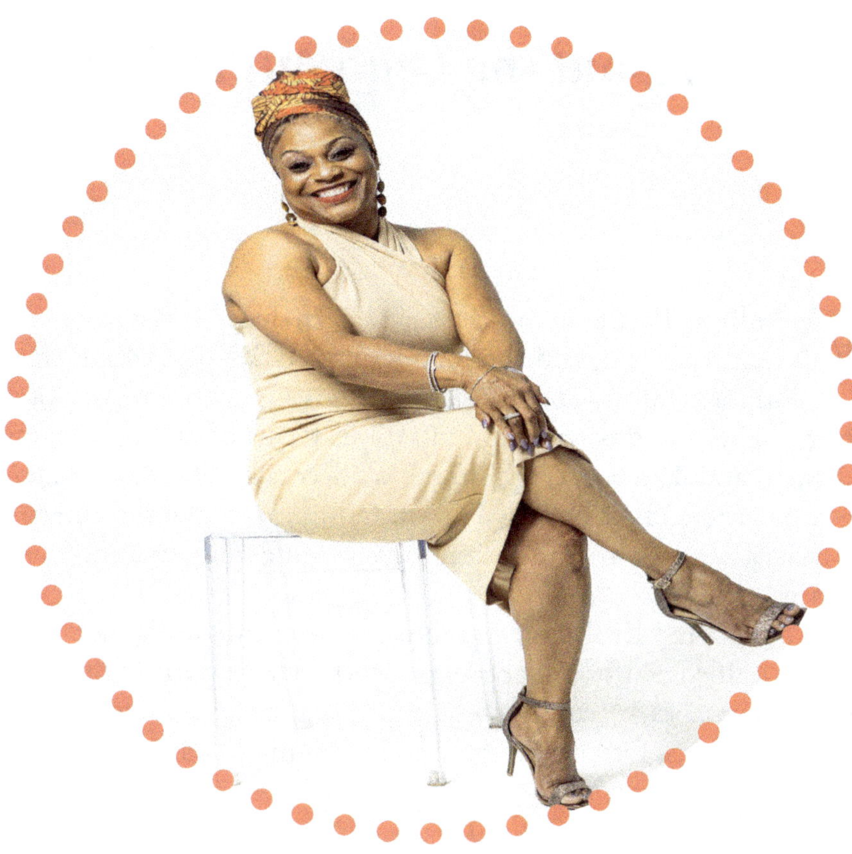

Amirah Palmer

Facebook: @Amirah Palmer | Instagram: @itsamirahpalmer

"About the Lead Author"

Amirah Palmer is not just a skater; she is a visionary, serial entrepreneur, and the founder and CEO of Sk8rz Konnect. Her platform, Sk8rz Konnect, serves as a showcase for the diverse skills and artistry found in various forms of skating, including roller, ice, and skateboarding. Amirah is a decorated U.S. Army Veteran, an International Best Selling Author, and a graduate of the University of Maryland. Her passion extends to volunteering and community service.

Through The Evolution of Skating series, Amirah Palmer aims to create a unified platform that brings together every genre of the skating arts. Her goal is to connect, showcase, and inspire skaters in their respective fields, fostering a sense of community and encouragement within the skating world.

www.ingramcontent.com/pod-product-compliance
Lightning Source LLC
LaVergne TN
LVHW010607110826
845149LV00003B/810

* 9 7 9 8 9 9 0 4 9 7 5 1 1 *